Cooking
with
Cheese

Cookery Adviser: Jane Grigson

Cooking with Cheese

Mary Berry

Illustrations by Laura Potter

B T Batsford London

My special thanks to Clare Blunt for her meticulous recipe development work in this book. My thanks also to both our families who have done a great deal of tasting.

First published 1980
© Mary Berry 1980

ISBN 0 7134 1925 3

Printed in Great Britain by
Redwood Burn Ltd,
Trowbridge & Esher
for the Publishers
B. T. Batsford Ltd,
4 Fitzhardinge Street,
London W1H 0AH.

Contents

Introduction

A piece of cheese fell on to a hot stone beside primitive man's camp fire. It bubbled and smelled good. He dipped a finger into it and licked it. It tasted good too – the first Welsh rarebit. The art of cheese cookery was born.

It may or may not have happened like this but we do know that cheese was eaten as long ago as 9000 BC. As soon as man stopped living entirely by hunting and became a herdsman, he discovered how to make cheese with the surplus milk from his cattle. Cheese was portable, it was nourishing, and it was good to eat. It has been made and eaten in most countries of the world ever since.

There are many references to it in the Bible. The classical Greeks loved it; it travelled with the armies of the Roman Empire throughout the known world. The monks in the medieval monasteries refined it and developed the more sophisticated cheeses – Brie, Camembert, Port Salut.

Until the present century cheeses were made in farmhouses, where milk was at hand. Farmhouse cheeses are still made – and much sought after – but with a growing population and increasing demand, cheesemaking has today become a large-scale industry and the vast majority of our cheeses come from factories. But all the individual characteristics remain and one type of cheese differs from another as – well, cheese from cheese. A particular cheese belongs essentially to the country in which it is made. Camembert cannot be made in England, nor Stilton in France. Each country then has its own distinct product and no one knows just how many there are. Here are a few of the ones we know and use today.

From France: Brie, Boursin, Camembert, Petit Suisse, Port Salut, Rocquefort. England makes Caerphilly, Cheddar, Cheshire (red, white and blue), Derby, Double Gloucester, Lancashire, Leicester, Stilton (blue and white), Wensleydale. Add to these the soft, creamy Highland cheeses of Scotland. From Italy come Bel Paese, Dolcellate, Gorgonzola, Mozzarella, Parmesan, Ricotta. Well known from the Netherlands are Edam and Gouda; and Emmenthal and Gruyère from Switzerland.

With this bewildering variety to choose from, what is the best cheese for cooking?

First, why cook with cheese at all? It is a perfect food in itself, full of nourishment and flavour, easy to digest. Bread and cheese has been a stable diet for centuries. Or take the ordinary cheese sandwich which used to be a joke – a bad one – with bread curling at the edges and stale cheese, in railway station buffets. But make it of good Cheddar, fresh sliced bread and butter, then toast it under the grill, serve it with lettuce, tomato, pickle . . . this is already a meal.

That is cooking with cheese.

In sauces, sprinkled on a dish, as a topping crisped under the grill or in the oven, it brings a flavour that nothing else can match. It adds nourishment and it transforms basic ingredients. It contributes to the great dishes of the world.

So what cheese should you use for cooking? The simple answer to that is to use the ones you like best, the ones that please your family's taste, the ones you have in stock. For example, Parmesan is the cheese the Italians heap lavishly on all forms of pasta. You can, if you like, use a well-flavoured Cheddar finely grated with your spaghetti. So don't be bound too much by tradition or by the recipe. One cheese can usually be substituted for another, provided you stick to the basic type. You would not, for instance, use Stilton instead of a soft cream cheese in a cheesecake mixture!

Cheddar is the great all-purpose cooking cheese. Use a well-flavoured one and grate it finely for sauces and toppings, for adding to pastry or scone mixes. Don't use one that is too mild in flavour or the dish will be bland and uninteresting. And remember that cheese is apt to be salty, so do not overseason the dish.

Any of the hard cheeses such as Cheshire, Lancashire or Parmesan can be substituted for or mixed with Cheddar. Use what you have in stock. A lot of cooks like to keep a supply, ready grated, made up of the odds and ends in the fridge. Gouda, Emmenthal and Gruyère melt easily and are good for cooking. Cream and cottage cheese go well in salads and are essential for mousses and creamy fillings for tartlets or cheesecake. Processed cheese and ready sliced cheese are useful for quick, mild-flavoured dishes.

Cook cheese as briefly as possible on a gentle heat. Too much cooking can make it tough or stringy. Serve it as soon as it is ready. Don't forget that cheese and wine or beer were made for each other, and are often served together. Wine or beer can also be added when you cook, such as wine in fondue and beer in a Welsh rarebit mixture.

How to buy cheese

The ideal is to buy from a specialist shop or delicatessen where the proprietor knows and understands the cheese he is selling. He will let you taste before you buy and advise you on your choice, so that you can add to your own knowledge. It is worth seeking out a shop like this, if only for special purchases.

Unfortunately we do not all have the opportunity to buy in this way. The corner shop where whole cheeses were cut into according to the customer's requirement is now largely a thing of the past. Most of us have to do our day-to-day buying from a suppermarket counter where the cheese is already cut and packed and neatly displayed by a staff who need know very little about what they are selling. However there are good supermarkets where you can sample the cheese before you buy it.

If you are buying cut Cheddar wrapped in film, as it is in most supermarkets, examine it as carefully as you can. See that it looks fresh and is without cracks or signs of sweating or oiliness. Experience is the best teacher here. The soft French cheeses present a bigger problem. Many are sold wrapped in foil and there is no chance of examining them. Buy these, if you can, from a specialist shop. They are more difficult to keep than the hard domestic cheeses and once they are ripe they have a short life. Buy only what you need at any one time.

This applies to a greater or lesser extent to all cheeses. Aim for a quick turn-over and use up left-over odds and ends of hard cheese by grating them together and either storing in the freezer or sprinkling over hot vegetables.

How to store cheese

Although it is always wise to buy cheese in small quantities, especially soft ones like Camembert, or the blue-veined Rocquefort type, many cheeses can be satisfactorily stored, with just a little care. Hard or semi-hard varieties, wrapped in waxed papers or foil, will keep in a cool larder for days or even weeks; or in a polythene bag loosely folded over at the neck in the refrigerator, but take them out about an hour before serving.

Cheeses such as Brie or Camembert should not be put in the fridge. Their storage time is two or three days at the most.

Freezing cheese

Freezing is another matter. The hard cheeses – Cheddar, Double Gloucester, Gouda – freeze well and will keep satisfactorily for up to four months. But they do tend to crumble when thawed and, after freezing for a month or so are better used for cooking. Grated cheese freezes very well and keeps for up to four months. Grated Parmesan, frozen, keeps for up to four years.

Rich cheeses – Brie, Camembert, Stilton – freeze successfully and keep for up to three months. Do be sure that they are in perfect ripe condition before freezing, and thaw thoroughly and completely before using.

Freezing dishes cooked with cheese

Quiches and flans freeze well. They are best thawed, then reheated and served hot; this crispens the pastry as well as bringing out the flavour of the cheese. Pasta freezes well in a combination dish such as Lasagne, Noodle layer and canneloni. Pizzas are best served hot so always reheat before serving, if need be without thawing first.

Slimming with cheese

We are nearly all, at some time in these diet-consious days, slimmers. The only difference is that some of us are more dedicated than others – those of us probably who have most to lose.

Cheese is, above all others, the slimmer's food. If you merely wish to cut down on what you eat, it is the ideal food for you. It is concentrated, it is big nourishment in small bulk, and small amounts of it yield a big proportion of our daily health needs. It is essential to include an adequate amount of high protein food in a slimming diet and cheese is an important source of protein.

If you think about it, it is unusual to eat more than a few ounces of cheese at a time. So cheese *in itself* should not upset your diet. It is what you eat and drink with it that does. This is why the experts recommend you to eat it along with other non-fattening foods, to make it part of a calorie-controlled diet, the one sure way of losing weight. All foods supply calories and the reason why people are overweight is that they eat more calories in food than their bodies can use up in energy. Slimming diets are designed to reduce the daily intake of calories.

It is important to distinguish between a low-fat diet and a calorie-controlled diet. They are not necessarily the same thing. Certain cheeses are low in fat as well as in calories. For this reason cottage cheese is the slimmer's best friend. It is made of skimmed milk, with very little fat remaining, and is not as high in food value as most cheeses. There are, of course, many other low-fat cheeses – Gouda and Edam are particularly good. Cream cheese, which is often virtually solidified double cream, obviously has the highest fat content and the highest number of calories. Here is a guide to the calorie content of some cheeses.

Cheese	Calories per 25g (oz)	Cheese	Calories per 25g (oz)
Cottage	33	Emmenthal	113
Camembert	88	Parmesan	118
Brie	88	Cheddar	120
Gouda	96	Cream	130
Blue	103		

If you are making a determined attempt to lose weight, there is no need to be miserable about it – you won't lose any more that way. Even a strictly controlled diet need not be boring. For instance, salad with cottage cheese is the slimmer's stand-by. Make it interesting by ringing the changes. Try cottage cheese with a fresh peach – it goes beautifully with fruits of all kinds, and with fresh, crisp vegetables such as celery or chicory, or with shredded cabbage. If you are making sandwiches, spread the bread with cottage cheese or one of the low-calorie cheese spreads that are on the market. At 33 or 72 calories to the ounce (25g) this is a very big saving on butter at a staggering 226.

When you are cooking fish, meat or vegetable dishes, a little grated cheese sprinkled on top will add few calories but lots of flavour and interest.

In a word, use cheese in your cooking, enjoy eating it and you will enjoy losing weight.

Note

One pint, a half and a quarter pint have been referred to in this book as 20, 10 and 5 fluid ounces.

Snacks and Sandwiches

Think of a snack and you think of cheese. The essence of a snack is that it is quick to prepare, easy to eat and, above all, tempting. What other food so well fulfils these conditions?

What other food is, in fact, as accommodating? Cheese blends happily with eggs in a fluffy omelette for a light lunch, or with minced meat in the hearty beefburgers loved by children, and it makes satisfying toasted sandwiches. The beauty of cheese is that it accepts and enhances all sorts of savoury additions – ham, chicken, fish, bacon – and makes a feast out of the left-overs in the store cupboard.

There are recipes here to suit everyone's taste – the classic Welsh rarebit, the delicate soufflé omelette, three-decker sandwiches, picnic suggestions, and some real children's favourites. (Incidentally, the children will enjoy making up their own snacks – and it could be an introduction to the art of cookery.)

Go all out for flavour. Use strong Cheddar or a mixture of cheeses, depending on what you have in stock. Odds and ends of different varieties can be blended into toast toppings or sandwich fillings with the addition of mustard and a drop or two of Worcestershire sauce.

There is no need of being afraid to experiment. Cheese gives you a chance to be adventurous and to satisfy your friends and family at the same time.

French cheese omelette   *Serves 1*

Choose a moist well-flavoured Cheddar cheese for omelettes. For colour add strips of skinned tomato flesh first, tossed in a little hot melted butter and seasoned.

2 large eggs
1 tbsp water
salt
freshly ground black pepper
12½g (½ oz) butter
40g (1½ oz) moist full-flavoured
  Cheddar cheese

Place the eggs, water and seasoning in a bowl and beat lightly with a fork. Heat the omelette pan over a medium heat until very hot, add the butter and when hot and frothy pour in the egg mixture. Using a fork, quickly draw mixture from the sides of the pan to the centre to allow uncooked egg to run underneath, shake pan and leave for a few seconds. Draw the pan from the heat and loosen the sides. Sprinkle the cheese onto the omelette, then fold the omelette in three, tap the pan and slip onto a warm plate and serve at once.

Fried cheese toasts   *Serves 3*

Fried sandwiches need to be served the moment that they come from the pan, when the cheese has just melted.

butter
12 thin slices bread
175g (6 oz) mild-flavoured
  Cheddar cheese, grated
4 level tbsp chutney
fat or oil for frying

Butter the bread thickly and spread half of the cheese and chutney on four slices of bread. Top each with a slice of bread and spread with remaining cheese and chutney and then place remaining bread, buttered side down, on top. Trim off the crusts and cut each into three fingers. Heat the fat or oil in a frying pan, add the sandwiches and fry until golden brown, turning once.

    Lift out and drain on kitchen paper and serve at once with tomato wedges.

Cheese rolls   *Makes 6*

Lovely served with home-made soup. For a change add freshly chopped chives to the grated cheese.

6 thin slices white bread
unsalted butter
50g (2 oz) full-flavoured Cheddar
  cheese, finely grated
25g (1 oz) butter, melted

Heat the oven to 200°C (400°F), gas mark 6.

    Butter the bread with the unsalted butter and trim off the crusts and then sprinkle the buttered surface with the cheese. Roll up each slice firmly like a Swiss roll and place on a baking sheet. Brush each roll with a little melted butter and bake in the oven for about 15 minutes or until crisp and golden brown.

Crispy bacon rolls *Makes 8*

Let the children prepare these for themselves – they are fun to do and
quickly disappear.

4 slices white bread
soft butter
50g (2 oz) full-flavoured Cheddar
   cheese, finely grated
4 rashers streaky bacon

Remove the crusts from the bread and then roll with a rolling pin to
flatten. Spread with the butter and sprinkle with grated cheese and then
firmly roll up each slice like a Swiss roll and cut in half to make eight rolls.
   Remove the rind from the bacon and spread flat with the back of a knife
and then wrap a piece of bacon around each bread roll and secure with a
wooden cocktail stick. Grill under a moderate heat for about 5 minutes,
turning frequently until the bacon is brown and the cheese is starting to
melt in the centre.

Cheese and potato cakes *Serves 3*

A firm favourite with all children for high tea.

225–350g (8–12 oz) mashed potato
   or 1 packet of instant for 2 to 3
   servings
150ml (5 fl. oz) boiling water (for the instant potato)
1 egg, beaten
50g (2 oz) mild-flavoured Cheddar
   cheese, finely grated
salt and pepper
brown bread crumbs
lard or dripping for frying
3 fried eggs

If using instant mashed potato make up as directed on the packet but using
only 150ml (5 fl. oz) of water to make the mash stiffer than usual. Cool and
then beat in the egg and cheese with plenty of seasoning. Divide the
mixture into six, shape into cakes and lightly coat in brown breadcrumbs.
   Heat the lard or dripping in a frying pan and fry the cakes for about 5
minutes, turning once until crisp and golden brown. Lift out and serve
with a fried egg.

Buck rarebit   *Serves 4*

Cheesey toast topped with a poached egg. Traditionally buck rarebit is
made with a crumbly cheese such as Lancashire or Cheshire, but you can
make it with Cheddar. There is no need to butter the toast as the cheese
mixture is rich enough without.

225g (8 oz) Lancashire cheese
2 eggs, beaten
1 tsp made English mustard
pepper
4 slices of bread, toasted
4 poached eggs

Crumble the cheese into a bowl and add the eggs, mustard and pepper and
mix well. Divide the mixture between the slices of toast and put under a
hot grill for 3 to 4 minutes or until the cheese is golden brown and bubbly.

   Place on a warm serving dish, put a poached egg on top of each and
serve at once.

Egg and cheese potato rolls   *Makes 10–12*

My children love these served with a couple of rashers of bacon and some
tomato ketchup.

675g (1½ lb) potatoes
6 hard-boiled eggs, chopped
1 tbsp finely grated raw onion
75g (3 oz) full-flavoured Cheddar
  cheese, grated
salt and pepper
2 eggs
4 tsp water
50g (2 oz) fresh white breadcrumbs
fat or oil for deep frying

Boil the potatoes until tender and then drain and mash well, stir in the
chopped hard-boiled eggs, onion, cheese and seasoning. Beat the two eggs
with the water and add just sufficient to the potato to moisten and then
shape into 10 to 12 rolls.

   Coat with the remaining beaten egg and then coat in the breadcrumbs.
Deep fry in hot fat or oil for about 4 minutes, turning once until golden
brown and hot through, lift out and drain on kitchen paper. Serve hot.

Welsh rarebit   *Serves 4*

The success of this snack is in the slow cooking over a low heat until the cheese has melted.

25g (1 oz) butter
175g (6 oz) full-flavoured Cheddar
   cheese, grated
1 tbsp beer
½ level tsp made English mustard
salt and pepper
4 slices hot toast

Melt the butter in a saucepan. Add the cheese, beer, mustard and seasoning and stir over a very low heat until the cheese has melted and the mixture is smooth.

  Place the slices of toast on the grill pan and spoon the mixture on top of each slice. Place under a hot grill to brown quickly and then serve at once. It is quite a good idea to line the grill pan with a piece of foil to catch any mixture that runs off the sides of the toast so that none is wasted.

Hawaiian snacks   *Makes 4*

This is a quick and easy snack to make from ingredients in the store cupboard.

4 slices bread
butter
4 pineapple rings
cinnamon, optional
Wensleydale or Cheshire cheese

Heat the grill to hot and lightly toast the bread on both sides, then trim off the crusts. Butter the toasts and place a pineapple ring on each slice and if liked sprinkle with a little cinnamon. Cut the cheese in slices and then into eight strips about 7.5cm (3 in.) by 1.25cm (½ in.) and lay two strips across the top of the pineapple ring. Return to the grill and allow the cheese to melt and turn lightly brown. Serve piping hot.

Cheese scotch eggs *Makes 4*

Served either hot or cold, these make a pleasant change from the usual
sausagemeat variety.

4 hard-boiled eggs
450g (1 lb) cooked hot potatoes
100g (4 oz) full-flavoured Cheddar
  cheese, grated
salt and pepper
a little beaten egg
breadcrumbs
fat or oil for deep frying

Shell the eggs. Mash the potatoes until smooth and free from all lumps and
then beat in the cheese and seasoning. It is not necessary to add any extra
milk or butter. Divide the mixture into four equal portions and then mould
each portion around an egg firmly until completely covered then dip each
in beaten egg and coat in breadcrumbs.

    Fry in hot deep fat or oil for about 3 minutes or until golden brown, lift
out and drain on kitchen paper and leave to cool slightly, before cutting in
half to serve.

Tomato cheeseburgers *Makes 6*

A great favourite for high tea or a snack meal.

225g (8 oz) raw minced beef
1 onion, finely chopped
½ can condensed tomato soup
salt and pepper
¼ level tsp mixed dried herbs
75g (3 oz) full-flavoured Cheddar
  cheese, grated
3 soft rolls or baps

Place the minced beef and onion in a saucepan and cook very slowly to
allow the fat to run out, then increase the heat and fry quickly to brown.
Stir in the tomato soup, seasoning and herbs and cook over a low heat for
25 to 30 minutes. Remove from the heat and stir in 50g (2 oz) cheese, taste
and check seasoning.

    Cut the rolls in half and toast the cut side under a moderate grill. Divide
the mixture between the rolls and sprinkle the remaining cheese on top of
the meat, return to the grill for a further 5 minutes or until the cheese is
melted and golden brown.

Triple decker sandwiches   *Makes 12*

For a variation replace the ham with thinly sliced roast beef, chicken or smoked salmon.

2 slices white bread
soft butter
2 slices ham
2 slices brown bread
25g (1 oz) cream cheese
sliced cucumber

Spread a slice of white bread with butter and cover with a layer of ham. Spread a slice of brown bread with butter and place butter-side down on top of the ham and spread the bread with cream cheese and cover with a layer of cucumber and ham.

   Spread a second slice of white bread with butter and put on top of the cucumber, butter-side down, then spread the other side with butter and cover with the other slice of ham. Butter the remaining slice of brown bread and place butter-side down on top of the ham. Press the sandwich together firmly and cut off all the crusts. Cut the sandwich into 12 cubes and spike each cube on a cocktail stick and top with a small slice of cucumber.

Sausage roll-ups   *Serves 4*

An ideal snack or high tea recipe, served with baked beans for the children or a large spoonful of chutney for adults.

450g (1 lb) pork sausages
100g – 175g (4–6 oz) Cheddar
   cheese
4 rashers streaky bacon

Heat the grill.

   Slit each sausage lengthwise. Cut the cheese into eight fingers the size of the sausages and place inside the slits.

   Remove the rind from the bacon and stretch flat with the back of a knife. Cut in half and wrap each half around a sausage spiral fashion and secure with a cocktail stick – make sure that they are wooden! Place the sausages under the grill and cook slowly, turning frequently, until they are cooked through, about 20 minutes. Remove the cocktail sticks and serve hot.

Cheese squares *Serves 2*

Very popular with children, an ideal high tea dish that they can prepare for themselves and their friends on their own. Also a very good way of serving left-over cheese sandwiches from a picnic.

4 slices white bread
100g (4 oz) butter
175g (6 oz) full-flavoured Cheddar
  cheese, sliced
salt and pepper
2 eggs

Spread the bread with half of the butter and using the cheese make up sandwiches, then trim off the crusts and cut each sandwich into four squares. Put the seasoning and eggs into a shallow dish and beat well together. Melt the remaining butter in a frying pan.
  Dip each sandwich in the egg mixture to coat thoroughly and fry for about 3 minutes in the butter on each side until golden brown and crisp. Drain on kitchen paper and serve hot.

Hot cheese ramekins *Serves 6*

Good for Sunday supper, followed by a little pâte and toast.

25g (1 oz) butter
1 onion, finely chopped
50g (2 oz) streaky bacon, chopped
50g (2 oz) mushrooms, chopped
salt and pepper
6 tbsp milk
2 eggs, separated
175g (6 oz) full-flavoured Cheddar
  cheese, grated

Heat the oven to 190°C (375°F) gas mark 5.
  Melt the butter in a saucepan and add the onion and cook gently for 5 minutes, then add the bacon and mushrooms and cook for a further 5 minutes or until the fat has run out of the bacon. Season well.
  Lightly butter six ramekin dishes, place a spoonful of the bacon mixture in the bottom of each dish, after carefully draining with a slotted spoon.
  Place the milk, egg yolks and cheese in a saucepan and heat gently until the cheese has melted.
  Whisk the egg whites until stiff and then fold into the cheese mixture. Divide between the six dishes. Bake in the oven for 10 to 15 minutes or until mixture is well risen and golden brown. Serve at once.

Savoury beefburgers *Makes 8*

These are very simple to make and the slice of cheese in the centre gives them a lovely flavour. In the summer they may be cooked outdoors over a medium heat on a barbecue.

450g (1 lb) lean raw minced beef
1 tsp Worcestershire sauce
1 level tsp fresh chopped marjoram
1 level tsp salt
ground black pepper
4 slices Cheddar cheese

Blend the meat, Worcestershire sauce, marjoram and seasoning together. Lightly flour the hands, divide the mixture into eight balls and then flatten each shape into a beefburger about 7.5cm (3 in.) in diameter. Sandwich the beefburgers together in pairs with a slice of cheese in the centre.

Place under a moderate grill for about 10 to 12 minutes, turning once until the beefburgers are cooked through and brown and the cheese in the centre has started to melt. Serve the beefburgers as they are for a snack, or for those who are hungry pop them into a soft bread roll or bap.

Cheesey porkburgers *Makes 8*

Minced pork makes a change from using the traditional beef and gives an excellent flavour with the cheese topping which gives a special lift to the recipe.

450g (1 lb) lean spare rib of pork
100g (4 oz) mushrooms
2 level tsp Dijon mustard
2 slices white bread, crusts
  removed
4 tbsp beer, ale or cider
1 level tsp salt
freshly ground black pepper
oil or lard for frying
4 baps, split
100g (4 oz) full-flavoured Cheddar
  cheese, grated

Trim the pork of any fat or skin and cut up into rough pieces and mince coarsely with the mushrooms into a large bowl, add the mustard and then put the bread through the mincer and add to the bowl with 3 tablespoons of the beer and seasoning. Mix together very thoroughly and then lightly flour the hands and shape the mixture into eight burgers. Heat the oil or lard in a frying pan and fry the burgers for about 10 minutes, turning once.

Meanwhile heat the grill and toast the baps on the outside.

Slowly melt the cheese in a small saucepan with the remaining beer.

Place a porkburger on each bap and spoon a little of the cheese mixture on top of each. Serve at once.

Savoury chicken tartlets *Makes 24*

An ideal way of using up a small quantity of cold chicken. These tartlets can be taken on a picnic or put in a packed lunch for a change.

Pastry
225 (8 oz) plain flour
50g (2 oz) margarine
50g (2 oz) lard
2 tbsp approx. cold water to mix

Filling
175g (6 oz) cooked chicken, finely
  chopped
2 sticks celery, finely chopped
100g (4 oz) full-flavoured Cheddar
  cheese, finely grated
5 tbsp mayonnaise, home-made (see
  p. 92) or a good bought variety
salt and pepper

Heat the oven to 190°C (375°F), gas mark 5. Make the pastry as for Watercress and Cheddar quiche (page 48). Roll out thinly and line 24 tart tins.

   Put the filling ingredients in a bowl and mix thoroughly, seasoning well, and then divide the mixture between the tarts. Bake in the oven for 30 minutes until the pastry is a pale golden colour at the edges, and serve either hot or cold.

Prawn tartlets

Make as above but use 175g (6 oz) peeled prawns, chopped, instead of the chicken, and 2 rounded tablespoons peas instead of the celery.

Ham tartlets

Make as for chicken tartlets but use 175g (6 oz) finely chopped lean ham instead of the chicken and 2 rounded tablespoons well-drained sweetcorn instead of the celery. Just before baking sprinkle the top with a little paprika.

Potted Cheddar

Used for sandwiches or for toast toppings, and keeps in the 'fridge for up to 2 weeks.

100g (4 oz) butter, softened
salt and pepper
1 level tsp made English mustard
225g (8 oz) full-flavoured Cheddar
  cheese, grated
3 tbsp approx. mayonnaise
1 tsp Worcestershire sauce

Place the butter in a bowl with plenty of salt and pepper and the mustard and beat thoroughly, then gradually work in the cheese, mayonnaise and Worcestershire sauce. Turn into a small bowl or dish, cover with a piece of foil and chill well before serving.

Croque monsieur   *Serves 4*

These hot sandwiches are very good and provide an ideal snack for a hungry family. You can use slices of processed Cheddar cheese for this, the flavour is usually stronger than a good cheddar.

8 square slices white bread,
  buttered
4 slices ham
4 slices Cheddar cheese
6 tbsp oil
50g (2 oz) butter for frying

Remove the crusts from the bread and on four slices place a slice of ham and a slice of cheese. Cover with the second slice of bread butter side down and trim the sides evenly. Cut each sandwich in half for easy handling.
   Heat the oil and butter in a large frying pan and when hot fry the sandwiches until lightly brown, then turn and brown the other side. Drain well on kitchen paper and serve hot at once with a good chutney.

Swiss eggs   *Serves 2*

Made in individual dishes it is easy to adapt this recipe for any number of people. They also make a very smart first course for a dinner party when one egg per person is sufficient and then they may be baked in ramekin dishes.

butter
4 eggs
4 tbsp double cream
salt
freshly ground black pepper
50g (2 oz) Gruyère cheese, grated

Heat the oven to 180°C (350°F), gas mark 4. Thoroughly butter two individual gratin dishes.

   Crack 2 eggs into each dish and spoon a tablespoon of cream over each egg. Season well and sprinkle the cheese around each egg over the white. Bake in the oven for 15 to 20 minutes or until the whites are set and the yolk is still soft. Serve at once in the dish with French bread and butter.

Cheese soufflé omelette   *Serves 2*

An excellent light lunch dish that can be made very quickly if unexpected guests call.

3 large eggs
1 tbsp cold water
salt
freshly ground black pepper
2 level tbsp grated Parmesan
  cheese
12½g (½ oz) butter

Separate the eggs and place the yolk in a basin with the water, seasoning and cheese and beat until pale and creamy.

   Whisk the egg whites using a rotary or electric whisk until just stiff.

   Mix one tablespoonful into the yolks and then carefully fold in the remainder.

   Heat the pan and then melt the butter in it over a moderate heat. Spread the mixture into the pan and cook without moving over a low heat for 3 to 4 minutes until a pale golden brown underneath. Slip under a medium grill for 2 to 3 minutes to set the top. Make a slight cut across the centre of the omelette, fold in half and slide onto a warm dish. Serve at once with a tossed green salad and fresh warm bread if you have some.

Rosy tuna ramekins   *Serves 4*

Serve hot with spinach or green beans for a quick snack lunch.

4 hard-boiled eggs
25g (1 oz) butter
25g (1 oz) flour
300ml (10 fl. oz) milk
2 tbsp tomato ketchup
salt and pepper
198g (7 oz) can tuna fish, drained and flaked
50g (2 oz) full-flavoured Cheddar cheese, grated

Cut the eggs in half lengthways and place two cut-side down in four individual ovenproof dishes.

Melt the butter in a pan and stir in the flour and cook for a minute, then blend in the milk and bring to the boil, stirring until thickened and simmer for 2 minutes. Add the ketchup, seasoning and tuna fish with 25g (1 oz) cheese and mix well. Spoon the mixture over the eggs and then sprinkle with the remaining cheese. Grill until golden brown and bubbling.

American toasted sandwiches   *Serves 4*

A great favourite with the men, quickly made from ingredients in the store cupboard, which may be varied to suit yourself.

75g (3 oz) butter
4 rashers streaky bacon
100g (4 oz) mushrooms, sliced
8 slices white bread
2 tbsp chutney
4 slices Cheddar cheese
1 tomato, sliced
parsley to garnish

Melt a small knob of butter in a saucepan, cut the rind and bone from the bacon and cut in small strips and fry with the mushrooms in the butter until golden brown and any fat has run out. Lift out with a slotted spoon. Meanwhile, heat the grill.

Butter the slices of bread and make up sandwiches, using the bacon and mushroom mixture with the chutney. Lightly toast on one side under the grill, then turn over and top each sandwich with a slice of cheese and slice of tomato. Return to the grill and toast until the cheese has started to melt and turns a pale golden brown. Remove and serve at once, garnished with a small sprig of parsley.

Soups and starters.

The good hostess gives a lot of thought to the first course. For a dinner party it must not be too heavy and filling – it is essential to remember the main course that is to come.

Serve something light and well-flavoured to tempt the appetite, something colourful to tempt the eye. An interesting first course, preferably served in individual dishes, can be prepared well in advance. Try a combination of cheese with prawns, cheese with tomatoes, with mushrooms, or with a smoked mackerel pâté. Use grated Cheddar, or make a pâté rich and smooth with cream cheese. Cottage cheese goes well with tomatoes. Many dinner party starters can be made in larger quantities and served as a main dish for lunch or supper.

Soups as a first course should be light; as the main part of a meal they should be thick and nourishing. In either case the addition of grated cheese makes a world of difference. The classic French onion soup would be unthinkable without it. Use Parmesan or Gruyère if possible, but grated Cheddar is a perfectly satisfactory substitute. Cheese croûtes – small cubes of bread in toasted cheese mixture – are a delightful savoury addition to soups.

Light, airy and easy to eat, soufflés and mousses are ideal first courses which, served with salad and fresh crusty bread, make perfect main dishes for lunch or supper. Vary them as you wish, with the addition of fish, vegetables, herbs, anything you have in stock. Curd cheese makes a mousse particularly smooth and creamy.

Mousses are made in advance and chilled before serving, but soufflés, in all their puffed-up golden glory, *must* come to the table the moment they are ready. So be sure your guests are ready too. It is wise to serve a soufflé for a small number of people so that it is not kept waiting.

Contrary to popular belief, soufflés are not difficult to make. The general principles are simple and straightforward but it is the timing that is important. The basic creamy sauce can be made in advance – in any case it has to be left to cool before the beaten egg whites are added. Be generous with flavouring at this stage – a mixture of strong Cheddar and Parmesan gives best results.

Remember that once the beaten egg whites have been folded in the soufflé must go into the oven immediately. It is imperative not to open the oven door while it is cooking. Time it carefully and have faith, and the result will delight you and your reputation as a cook will soar.

Tomatoes Lucinda   *Serves 6*

Wait for tomatoes to be really cheap in the height of summer to make this recipe and choose really firm ones.

12 tomatoes
175g (6 oz) soft curd cheese
150ml (5 fl. oz) soured cream
1 clove garlic, crushed
4 stuffed green olives, chopped
3 tsp chopped chives
4 tbsp French dressing

Put the tomatoes in a pan of boiling water for 10 seconds, drain and remove the skins. Cut a slice from the stem end of each tomato and remove the seeds with a teaspoon, leaving the tomato shells in one piece.

Blend together the cheese, soured cream, garlic, olives and 2 teaspoons of chopped chives and then spoon this mixture equally between the tomato cases.

Blend the remaining chives with the French dressing and spoon over the tomatoes just before serving. Serve 2 tomatoes per portion.

French onion soup   *Serves 4*

Well worth making, it is essential to fry the onions very slowly until a rich golden brown, which then gives an excellent flavour and colour to the soup.

25g (1 oz) butter
25g (1 oz) bacon fat
450g (1 lb) onions, very finely sliced
25g (1 oz) flour
900ml (1½ pts) stock or water
  using 2 beef stock cubes
salt and pepper
4 slices French bread
50g (2 oz) Gruyère cheese, grated

In a large saucepan melt the butter and bacon fat, add the onions and fry them very gently, stirring occasionally until golden brown. Stir in the flour and cook for a minute. Add the stock, bring to the boil, stirring, and simmer for 30 minutes; season to taste.

Toast one side of the French bread and then sprinkle the untoasted side with the cheese and put under a hot grill until the cheese has melted. Turn the soup into four bowls and float a slice of bread on each bowl of soup.

Smoked mackerel pâté   *Serves 6*

This pâté may also be made using smoked trout which gives a milder flavour.

2 smoked mackerel
275g (10 oz) butter, melted but not hot
100g (4 oz) cream cheese
juice of ½ a lemon
small sprigs of parsley or
  watercress to garnish

Remove the skin and bones from the mackerel and put the fillets with 225g (8 oz) of the butter, the cream cheese and the lemon juice in the blender in two batches and blend until smooth. Divide the pâté between six individual serving dishes and smooth the tops, or put in a small tureen or dish of about 600ml (1 pt) capacity.

    Remelt the remaining butter and pour a thin layer on top of each dish and leave in a cool place until set. Serve garnished with small sprigs of parsley or watercress and hot toast and butter.

Stuffed tomatoes with cottage cheese   *Serves 4 for a starter, or 2 for lunch*

A very attractive way of serving tomatoes which should ideally be large and firm. Serve either on individual plates, or for a light lunch in the centre of a salad platter.

4 large, firm tomatoes
100g (4 oz) cottage cheese
1 pickled sweet cucumber, chopped
1 tbsp sweet chutney, chopped
2 tbsp home-made mayonnaise
salt and pepper
punnet of cress to garnish

Skin the tomatoes by plunging them in boiling water for 10 seconds and then into cold water. It will then be easy to peel of the skins. Place the tomatoes, stalk down on a wooden board. With a small knife make cuts almost through to the base of the tomato to form six petals. Open out the petals to form a flower shape and carefully remove the seeds from the centre of the tomato. Repeat with the remaining tomatoes.

    Mix together the cottage cheese, cucumber, chutney, mayonnaise and seasoning and then divide the mixture between the tomatoes. Garnish with the cress.

Scallops in cider   *Serves 8*

Scallops make an ideal starter to a dinner party. Cider is less expensive than wine and for this recipe is just as good.

8 scallops or 450g (1 lb) packet
  frozen scallops, thawed
1 small onion, finely chopped
1 stick celery, chopped
1 sprig thyme
1 bayleaf
450ml (15 fl. oz) dry cider
40g (1½ oz) butter
40g (1½ oz) flour
salt and pepper
675g (1½ lb) potatoes, cooked and
  mashed
75g (3 oz) full-flavoured Cheddar
  cheese

Put the scallops in a pan with the onion, celery, thyme, bayleaf and cider and simmer gently for 5 minutes or until the scallops are tender, then lift the scallops from the pan and cut into two or three pieces and strain the cooking liquor and retain.

Melt the butter in a saucepan, add the flour and cook for a minute, remove the pan from the heat and stir in the cooking liquor, return to the stove and bring to the boil, stirring until thickened. Add the scallops and season well.

Pipe a border of mashed potato around the edge of eight scallop shells or individual serving dishes and lightly brush the top with a little melted butter. Divide the scallop mixture between the shells and sprinkle the top with grated cheese. Re-heat in a hot oven 200°C (400°F), gas mark 6 for 20 to 25 minutes or until piping hot and golden brown.

Prawns in scallop shells   *Serves 4*

Prawns are a luxury now but go a long way in this recipe when blended with tomatoes and eggs.

450g (1 lb) potatoes, cooked and
  mashed
25g (1 oz) butter
25g (1 oz) flour
300ml (10 fl. oz) milk
salt and pepper

50g (2 oz) full-flavoured Cheddar
  cheese, grated
2 hard-boiled eggs, sliced
4 tomatoes, peeled and sliced
100g (4 oz) prawns

Pipe or fork the mashed potato around the edge of four scallop shells or individual dishes.

    Melt the butter in a saucepan and add the flour and cook for 2 minutes, stir in the milk and bring to the boil and simmer until thickened, season well and stir in the cheese until melted.

    Divide the slices of hard-boiled eggs and tomatoes between the scallop shells and then cover with the prawns. Spoon over the cheese sauce.

    When required bake in a moderate oven 190°C (375°F), gas mark 5 for 20 to 25 minutes until hot through and potato is browned.

Cheese and prawn ramekins *Serves 4*

An easy first course that could also be made in one large dish and served for lunch.

40g (1½ oz) butter
100g (4 oz) button mushrooms,
  sliced
3 hard-boiled eggs
12½g (½ oz) flour
150ml (5 fl. oz) milk
50g (2 oz) full-flavoured Cheddar
  cheese, grated
100g (4 oz) peeled prawns
salt and pepper

Melt 25g (1 oz) butter in a small saucepan, add the mushrooms and cook gently for 5 minutes or until tender. Roughly chop the eggs.

    Melt the remaining butter in a pan, stir in the flour and cook for a minute, blend in the milk and bring to the boil, stirring until thickened, and simmer for 2 minutes. Add the eggs, prawns, mushrooms and 25g (1 oz) of cheese and season well. Divide the mixture between four individual serving dishes or ramekins, sprinkle over the remaining cheese and brown under a hot grill.

Family soup   *Serves 4–6*

A good main meal soup, served with rolls or French bread. Vary the vegetables according to what is in season or you have to hand.

397g (14 oz) can peeled tomatoes
600ml (1 pt) good stock
2 carrots, finely diced
2 onions, chopped
1 leek, finely sliced
2 sticks celery, chopped
1 small cauliflower, broken in small florets
salt and pepper
¼ small cabbage, finely shredded
Parmesan cheese

Place all the ingredients, except the cabbage and cheese in a large saucepan and bring to the boil, cover and simmer for about 40 minutes or until all the vegetables are tender, stir in the cabbage and continue cooking for a further 15 minutes.

Taste and check seasoning, pour into a hot soup tureen and sprinkle the top with plenty of Parmesan cheese and serve piping hot.

Chilled tuna ramekins   *Serves 4*

A different beginning, served with granary bread and unsalted butter.

Top

75g (3 oz) rich cream cheese	2 tsp lemon juice
1 rounded tbsp mayonnaise, home made (see page 92) or a good bought variety	5 tbsp water
	12½g (½ oz) gelatine

Base

198g (7 oz) can tuna fish, drained and flaked	4 rounded tbsp mayonnaise
50g (2 oz) cucumber, peeled and finely chopped	salt and pepper
1 spring onion, finely sliced	chopped fresh dill or parsley for decoration

To prepare the top, cream the cheese until smooth and then beat in the mayonnaise, lemon juice and one tablespoon of water until smooth.

Dissolve the gelatine in the remaining water by placing in a small cup or bowl and leaving to stand for 3 minutes to become a sponge, then standing over a pan of simmering water until melted and clear. Remove from the heat. Stir 2 teaspoons of the melted gelatine into the cream cheese mixture.

Now prepare the base by mixing all the ingredients together with plenty of seasoning and stirring in the remaining gelatine mixture. Divide between four ramekin dishes and smooth the mixture flat. Spoon the cream cheese mixture on top and put in the refrigerator for several hours to chill before serving. Decorate with chopped dill or parsley.

Cheese croûtes

Served with any of your favourite soups they make a lovely change.

25g (1 oz) finely grated cheese
12½g (½ oz) butter
salt and pepper
a little dry mustard power
a little cayenne pepper
1–2 rounds of white bread
  0.60–1.25cm (¼–½ oz) thick

Cream the cheese and butter together in a small bowl and add salt and pepper with the mustard and cayenne so that the mixture is well seasoned.
  Heat the grill, toast the bread on one side, turn over and spread the cheese mixture on the other side and return to the grill and toast until golden brown and bubbling.
  Trim the crusts and cut each slice into small cubes and serve at once.

Tomato appetizers *Serves 6*

Make this in the summer when tomatoes are at their cheapest. This is a good way of using up fairly small tomatoes and makes a good start to a meal.

12 small, firm tomatoes
75g (3 oz) Parmesan cheese, grated
salt
freshly ground black pepper
a little dried basil
150ml (5 fl. oz) double cream

Put the tomatoes in a bowl and cover with boiling water and leave to stand for 10 seconds, then drain and peel off the skins. Cut each tomato in half and then place four halves in individual soufflé dishes and sprinkle with some of the cheese, season well and sprinkle each dish with a little dried basil. Then sprinkle with the remaining cheese and pour a little cream over each dish. Place at the top of a moderate oven, 190°C (375°F), gas mark 5 for about 15 minutes so that the cheese has just turned pale golden brown. Serve hot with slices of French bread.

Hereford mousse   *Serves 6*

A light, easy starter. Serve with wafer-thin brown bread and butter.

1 small clove garlic
175g (6 oz) rich cream cheese
425g (15 oz) can consommé
1 tbsp sherry
1 level tsp curry powder
50g (2 oz) fresh prawns

Crush the garlic and place in a blender with the cheese, consommé, sherry and curry powder and mix well until smooth. Pour into six individual ramekins or dishes and leave in a cool place until set.

Just before serving arrange a few whole prawns on top of each mousse.

Heavenly egg mousse   *Serves 6*

A very versatile mousse, that can easily be turned into a fish and egg mousse by halving the eggs and adding approx. 175g (6 oz) either flaked fresh salmon or a can of salmon. As well as a first course this could be served as a lunch dish with French bread and a salad.

411g (14½ oz) can consommé
12½g (½ oz) gelatine
75g (3 oz) fresh curd cheese
300ml (10 fl. oz) home-made
  mayonnaise
6 eggs, hard-boiled
black pepper
150ml (5 fl. oz) soured cream
salt
a little lemon juice to taste
1 level tbsp chopped parsley

Put 5 tablespoons of the consommé into a cup, add the gelatine and leave to soak for 5 minutes. Stand the cup in a pan of simmering water and stir until the gelatine has dissolved, then stir into the remaining consommé. Put a quarter of the consommé on one side and then leave the remainder in a cool place until starting to set.

Blend the curd cheese with the mayonnaise in a large bowl. Chop the eggs, the easiest way is in a bowl with a potato masher and then stir into the mayonnaise with plenty of black pepper, soured cream and salt and lemon juice to taste. Stir in the partially set consommé. Turn into a 1 litre (2 pt) dish and leave to chill until set.

Blend the parsley with the remaining consommé and pour in a thin layer over the top of the mousse, return to the refrigerator and chill for a further half-hour before serving.

Cheese soufflé   *Serves 3–4*

If you can make a good white sauce you can generally make a soufflé. To keep the cost down you can use all cheddar cheese.

40g (1½ oz) butter
40g (1½ oz) flour
300ml (10 fl. oz) hot milk
salt and pepper
1 level tsp made English mustard
75g (3 oz) full-flavoured Cheddar
   cheese, grated
25g (1 oz) Parmesan cheese, grated
4 large eggs

Heat the oven to 190°C (375°F), gas mark 5 and place a thick, heavy baking sheet in it. Melt the butter in a pan, stir in the flour and cook for 2 minutes without browning. Remove the pan from the heat and stir in the hot milk. Return to the heat and bring to the boil, stirring until thickened, then add the seasoning and mustard and leave to cool. Stir in the cheese.

Separate the eggs and beat the yolks one at a time into the cheese sauce. Whisk the egg whites with a rotary hand or electric whisk until stiff but not dry. Stir one tablespoonful into the cheese sauce and then fold in the remainder carefully. Pour into a buttered, 1 litre (2 pt) soufflé dish, run a teaspoon around the edge – this makes the soufflé rise evenly and not spill over the sides of the dish. Bake on the hot baking sheet in the centre of the oven for about 40 minutes until well risen and golden brown. Serve at once.

Spinach and cheese soufflé   *Serves 3–4*

Using the cheese soufflé recipe above, add 450g (1 lb) cooked, finely chopped and well-drained spinach to the mixture before the egg yolks with a pinch of nutmeg. After putting in the dish sprinkle the top with 25g (1 oz) grated Parmesan cheese.

Pasta and rice

Cheese goes with pasta as tripe goes with onions. The Italians use Parmesan and this is undoubtedly the ideal. It has been a part of Italian cooking for at least 800 years and the flavour it gives to a dish is unique. It is used with all forms of pasta – spaghetti, macaroni, lasagne, canelloni and all their myriad variations. It is a natural companion to rice dishes too and an essential with risotto. But if necessary you can substitute a good full-flavoured Cheddar, finely grated. The one essential is cheese – and plenty of it.

Pasta provides a wide range of satisfying meals. It is economical too. At its simplest a dish of spaghetti, well-buttered and liberally sprinkled with grated cheese, served perhaps with a green salad, is a meal in itself. Add a good sauce, plenty of seasoning and herbs, with chopped ham and tomatoes – and you have a banquet.

Pasta and rice dishes are invaluable for using up left-over ham, chicken, sausage, the remains of the weekend joint. They can be made in advance and reheated when wanted; they also freeze well. If you have odds and ends of several different cheeses in the larder, try blending them for good flavour.

Vegetables such as mushrooms, tomatoes, spinach and onions are important ingredients, whilst tossed green salad is a welcome accompaniment.

Monday bake   *Serves 4–6*

A very good way of using up the last cuts of the Sunday joint.

100g (4 oz) noodles	225–350g (8–12 oz) cooked beef,
50g (2 oz) butter	pork, lamb or ham, diced
50g (2 oz) flour	225g (8 oz) cooked peas or carrots
600ml (1 pt) milk	100g (4 oz) full-flavoured Cheddar cheese, grated
150ml (5 fl. oz) cider	salt and pepper

Cook the noodles in fast-boiling salted water as directed on the packet or until tender, drain and rinse thoroughly in warm water then leave to drain again.

Melt the butter in a large saucepan, add the flour and cook for a minute, blend in the milk and bring to the boil, stirring until thickened and simmer for 2 minutes. Add the cider, meat, vegetables, noodles and half of the cheese to the saucepan, mix well and add plenty of seasoning. Turn into a shallow, 1.7 litre approx. (3 pt) ovenproof dish and sprinkle over the remaining cheese. Bake in the oven at 200°C (400°F), gas mark 6 for 25 to 30 minutes or until hot through and golden brown.

Macaroni cheese   *Serves 4*

Macaroni cheese always goes down well for a family lunch or high tea. For a change fold 100g (4 oz) cooked ham and a couple of chopped tomatoes into the sauce with the macaroni.

75g (3 oz) short-cut macaroni
25g (1 oz) butter
25g (1 oz) flour
450ml (15 fl. oz) milk
100g (4 oz) full-flavoured Cheddar or
   Double Gloucester cheese, grated
salt and pepper
6 rashers of streaky bacon

Cook the macaroni in fast-boiling salted water until tender, about 10 minutes or as directed on the packet. Drain thoroughly and put aside.

   Melt the butter in a saucepan, stir in the flour and cook for 1 minute over a low heat. Blend in the milk and bring to the boil, stirring until thickened, simmer for 2 minutes. Remove from the heat and stir in 75g (3 oz) of the cheese with plenty of seasoning, then add the macaroni and mix well. Pour into a lightly greased 1 litre (1¾ pt) ovenproof dish and sprinkle with the remaining cheese. When required put in a hot oven 220°C (425°F), gas mark 7 for about 20 minutes until golden brown.

   Remove the rind and bone from the bacon and cut each rasher in half, roll up and bake in the oven alongside the macaroni until browned. When ready to serve drain the bacon rolls and arrange on top of the macaroni and serve piping hot.

Spaghetti grill   *Serves 4*

This is a budget dish that goes well with a green salad.

100g (4 oz) spaghetti
salt
62½g (2½ oz) butter
2 large onions, chopped
175g (6 oz) streaky bacon, chopped
40g (1½ oz) flour
450ml (15 fl. oz) milk
freshly ground black pepper
100g (4 oz) full-flavoured Cheddar
  cheese, grated
½ level tsp mixed dried herbs
4 tomatoes, skinned and chopped

Cook the spaghetti in fast-boiling salted water as directed on the packet or until tender for about 10 to 12 minutes, rinse in warm water and drain thoroughly.

Melt 25g (1 oz) butter in a frying pan and then fry the onions and bacon for about 10 minutes or until cooked through.

Place the remaining butter in a saucepan and add the flour and cook for a minute. Blend in the milk and bring to the boil. stirring until thickened, and add half of the cheese, black pepper and dried herbs, cooking very gently for 2 minutes.

Combine the spaghetti, cheese sauce, tomatoes and stir in the bacon and onion mixture which should be lifted from the frying pan with a slotted spoon. Taste and check seasoning as the spaghetti will absorb quite a lot of salt. Turn into a shallow 1.7 litre approx. (3 pt) buttered ovenproof dish and sprinkle with the remaining cheese. Put under a medium grill for about 5 minutes or until the top is golden brown and bubbly.

Tuna bake   *Serves 4*

This dish may be made in advance or even on the day before required and then just re-heated. Tasty alternatives to tuna fish are chopped ham or bacon or a can of salmon.

175g (6 oz) spaghetti	100g (4 oz) full-flavoured Cheddar
salt	cheese, grated
62½g (2½ oz) butter	1 large onion, sliced
50g (2 oz) flour	200g (7 oz) can tuna fish, drained
600ml (1 pt) milk	and roughly flaked
freshly ground black pepper	2 hard-boiled eggs, roughly
½ level tsp made mustard	chopped

Cook the spaghetti in boiling salted water until tender, about 10 minutes. Drain thoroughly and rinse in warm water and then drain again.

Melt 50g (2 oz) butter in a saucepan, add the flour and cook for 1 minute. Gradually add the milk and bring to the boil, stirring frequently. Add 1 level teaspoon salt, pepper to taste and mustard and simmer for 2 minutes. Remove from the heat and stir in 75g (3 oz) of the cheese, until melted.

Fry the onion in the remaining butter until golden brown, then drain.

Lightly grease a 1.7 litre approx. (3 pt) ovenproof casserole and place half the spaghetti in it, pour over half the sauce, cover with the tuna fish, onions and chopped eggs. Finally lay the remaining spaghetti on top and pour over the rest of the sauce, then sprinkle with the remaining cheese. Cook in the oven at 200°C (400°F), gas mark 6 for about 1 hour or until hot through and the top is well browned.

Macaroni savoury   *Serves 4*

A quick dish to make, using for a change any cooked left-over meat, tuna fish or luncheon meat.

100g (4 oz) quick-cook macaroni
25g (1 oz) butter
1 large onion, chopped
298g (10½ oz) can condensed
   tomato soup
100g (4 oz) cooked ham, diced
75g (3 oz) full-flavoured Cheddar
   cheese, grated

Cook the macaroni as directed on the packet in plenty of fast-boiling salted water and drain well.

Melt the butter in a pan, add the onion and cook gently for about 10 minutes or until soft but not brown. Add the macaroni to the pan and toss lightly so that it is well coated with butter. Stir in the soup and ham and mix well, seasoning to taste if necessary. Turn into a shallow ovenproof dish and sprinkle over the cheese. Place under a hot grill until the cheese has melted and is golden brown and bubbling.

Noodle layer   *Serves 6*

If liked this dish may be prepared in the morning and re-heated from cold when it will need about 45 minutes in the oven.

450g (1 lb) lean pork
1 large onion, quartered
25g (1 oz) butter
25g (1 oz) flour
400g (14 oz) can tomatoes
1 clove garlic, crushed
Sauce
40g (1½ oz) butter
40g (1½ oz) flour
450ml (15 fl. oz) milk
½ level tsp made
   English mustard

½ level tsp mixed dried herbs
salt and pepper
900g (2 lb) fresh spinach, cooked
   and drained or 450g (1 lb) packet
   fresh chopped spinach
150g (5 oz) noodles

salt and pepper
50g (2 oz) full-flavoured Cheddar
cheese, grated
50g (2 oz) Emmenthal cheese, grated
12½g (½ oz) Parmesan cheese, grated

Trim any rind from the pork and mince with the onion. Melt the butter in a saucepan, add the pork and onion and fry for 10 minutes; stir in the flour then add the tomatoes, garlic, herbs and salt and pepper and mix well, cover the pan and reduce the heat and simmer for 30 minutes.

Meanwhile cook the spinach as directed on the packet and drain very well and then spread over the base of a 2.3 litre approx. (4 pt) ovenproof dish. Heat the oven to 190°C (375°F), gas mark 5.

Cook the noodles in fast-boiling salted water for about 7 minutes or as directed on the packet, rinse in warm water and drain well.

To make the sauce, melt the butter in a saucepan, add the flour and cook for a minute, blend in the milk and bring to the boil stirring until thickened, add the mustard and seasoning and cook for 2 minutes. Mix the Cheddar and Emmenthal cheese together and stir half into the sauce.

Pour half the sauce on top of the spinach, then cover with the noodles and spoon the meat sauce on top. Finally pour over the remaining sauce, sprinkle with the remaining cheeses and bake in the oven for 35 minutes or until golden brown and bubbling. Serve with a green salad.

Risotto Milanese   *Serves 4*

An easily made lunch or supper dish that needs only a green salad to go with it.

225g (8 oz) long-grain rice
4 rashers back bacon
1 small onion, chopped
40g (1½ oz) butter
600ml (1 pt) chicken stock
100g (4 oz) button mushrooms
100g (4 oz) full-flavoured Cheddar cheese
salt and pepper

Rinse the rice and drain thoroughly. Remove the rind from the bacon and cut into strips and put in saucepan with the onion and 25g (1 oz) of the butter and fry for about 5 to 10 minutes or until the onion is soft but not brown and any fat has run from the bacon. Stir in the rice and cook for a minute to allow it to absorb the butter, then add the stock and bring to the boil, stirring all the time. Cover with a lid, reduce the heat and simmer for about 20 to 30 minutes, stirring occasionally. The rice will then be tender and the stock absorbed. If the rice is still slightly firm add a little extra stock and cook for a few minutes more, the time varying with the variety of rice used.

Slice the mushrooms and fry in the remaining butter for a few minutes, stir into the rice with half the cheese using a fork and mix lightly. Taste and check seasoning and then turn into a warm dish and sprinkle the remaining cheese on top.

Quick Italian spaghetti   *Serves 4*

A quick supper dish which goes well with a tossed green salad. I also make this dish if I have spaghetti left after serving Spaghetti bolognaise. Then I reheat the spaghetti in boiling salted water for 2 minutes and then proceed as below.

225g (8 oz) spaghetti
100g (4 oz) streaky bacon or
   whatever you have in the fridge
12½g (½ oz) butter
175g (6 oz) button mushrooms, sliced
1 tbsp fresh chopped parsley
2 eggs, beaten
salt and pepper
25–50g (1–2 oz) grated Parmesan cheese

Cook the spaghetti in plenty of fast-boiling salted water for 10 to 12 minutes or as directed on the packet until tender, then drain well and return to the pan.

Whilst the spaghetti is cooking remove the rind and bone from the bacon and cut into strips. Melt the butter in a pan and fry the bacon until it is a pale golden brown. Add the mushrooms and cook for 2 minutes, then blend the bacon and mushroom mixture into the cooked spaghetti with the parsley, eggs, pepper and salt. Cook over a low heat, stirring with a fork until the eggs have scrambled. Pile onto a warm serving dish and sprinkle with the Parmesan cheese and serve at once.

Andalusian spaghetti   *Serves 4 as a starter or 2 as supper*

Really piquant spaghetti from ingredients that are often in the larder.

3 tbsp olive oil
225g (8 oz) button mushrooms, sliced
2 onions, thinly sliced
2 cloves garlic, crushed
5 anchovy fillets, halved
3 rashers back bacon, chopped
100g (4 oz) spaghetti
6 stuffed green olives, sliced
25g (1 oz) Parmesan cheese, grated
chopped parsley to garnish

Heat the oil in a heavy pan and gently cook the mushrooms, onions, garlic, anchovy fillets and bacon, stirring frequently for about 10 minutes or until the onion is tender.

Meanwhile cook the spaghetti in boiling salted water for 10 to 12 minutes until tender or as directed on the packet. Drain well.

Add the olives to the mixture in the pan.

Pile the spaghetti on a serving dish and top with the savoury mixture. Sprinkle with the cheese and parsley and serve at once.

Spanish rice   *Serves 4*

If you have difficulty in getting cocktail sausages, use pork chipolatas and give them an extra twist in the middle to make cocktail-sized ones.

175g (6 oz) long grain rice
1 tbsp oil
225g (8 oz) pork cocktail sausages
1 large onion, chopped
220g (7½ oz) can apricots, drained
  and chopped
200g (7 oz) can red peppers,
  drained and chopped
25g (1 oz) sultanas
½ level tsp salt
freshly ground black pepper
12 stuffed green olives, sliced
100g (4 oz) full-flavoured Cheddar
  cheese, cubed

Cook the rice in boiling salted water until just tender, for about 10 minutes, or as directed on the packet. Drain and rinse under warm water and keep warm.

Heat the oil and fry the sausages until browned and cooked, about 10 minutes. Drain on kitchen paper and keep hot. Add the onions to the fat remaining in the pan and fry until tender and lightly browned. Drain all excess fat and oil from the pan and then add all the ingredients except the olives and cheese and heat through stirring gently until well blended and hot through. Then stir in the cheese and olives and pile onto a serving dish. Serve with a green salad.

Canneloni filled with cranberries and ham   *Serves 4–5*

At Christmas time use left-over turkey instead of ham or mix the two. If you have no cream in the house use mayonnaise instead.

25g (1 oz) butter
1 large onion, chopped
225g (8 oz) ham, finely chopped
4 tbsp whole cranberry sauce

3 tbsp double cream
salt and pepper
10 sticks approx. 'no cook'
   canneloni

Cheese sauce
25g (1 oz) butter
25g (1 oz) flour
450ml (15 fl. oz) milk
1 level tsp made English mustard

salt and pepper
75g (3 oz) full-flavoured Cheddar
   cheese, grated

Heat the oven to 190°C (375°F), gas mark 5.

Melt the butter in a small pan and fry the onion until soft but not brown for about 10 minutes, add the ham, cranberries and cream and season well. Fill into the canneloni.

To make the sauce, melt the butter in a pan and stir in the flour and cook for a minute. Blend in the milk and bring the sauce to the boil, stirring until thickened and then simmer for 2 minutes. Add the mustard, seasoning and 50g (2 oz) of the cheese.

Place a little sauce in the base of a shallow ovenproof dish and lay the canneloni on top in a single layer and then pour over the remaining sauce. Sprinkle with the rest of the cheese and put in the oven and bake for about 35 to 40 minutes or until the top is golden brown and bubbling and the canneloni tender. Serve with a green vegetable and rolls or chunks of French bread.

Lasagne *Serves 6*

A classic meat and cheese dish, blending three different cheeses, gives the dish an excellent flavour.

Meat sauce

1 tbsp oil	90g (3½ oz) can tomato purée
450g (1 lb) minced beef	2 cloves garlic, crushed
25g (1 oz) streaky bacon, derinded and chopped	2 tsp redcurrant jelly
	1 beef stock cube
225g (8 oz) onions, chopped	½ tsp salt
4 sticks celery, chopped	pepper
12½g (½ oz) flour	¼ level tsp dried mixed herbs
300ml (10 fl. oz) water	

White sauce

40g (1½ oz) butter	½ tsp Dijon mustard
40g (1½ oz) flour	100g (4 oz) full-flavoured Cheddar cheese, grated
¼ tsp nutmeg	100g (4 oz) Emmenthal cheese, grated
salt and pepper	150g (5 oz) uncooked lasagne
600ml (1 pt) milk	12½g (½ oz) Parmesan cheese, grated

For the meat sauce, heat the oil in a pan, add the beef and bacon and fry until browned. Add the onions and celery and cook for 5 minutes, stir in the flour and the remaining sauce ingredients, stir well and bring to the boil, cover and simmer for 1 hour, stirring from time to time.

For the white sauce, melt the butter in a large pan and stir in the flour, nutmeg, salt and pepper and cook gently for 2 minutes. Remove the pan from the heat and gradually add the milk, stirring to make a smooth mixture. Return the pan to the heat and cook, stirring until the sauce has thickened, add the mustard and check seasoning.

Combine the Cheddar and Emmenthal cheeses.

In a shallow 2 litre (3½ pt) casserole put a third of the meat sauce, the white sauce, then a third of the mixed cheeses followed by half of the uncooked lasagne (lay edge to edge, not overlapping). This usually takes three pieces, but if necessary break to size. Then start again with a third of the meat sauce, white sauce and cheese and the last half of the lasagne. Repeat finishing with a layer of meat sauce, white sauce and cheese, then sprinkle with the Parmesan cheese.

Leave till cold, then cook at 180°C (350°F), gas mark 4 for about 45 minutes to 1 hour or until the top is golden brown and bubbling. Serve at once, or the lasange may be kept hot at 100°C (200°F) gas mark ¼ for up to an hour if necessary.

Spaghetti expresso *Serves 4*

A quick supper dish that is prepared and cooked in one pan and needs only a green salad to serve with it.

225g (8 oz) spaghetti
salt
2 eggs
25g (1 oz) Parmesan cheese, grated
50g (2 oz) Cheddar cheese, grated
225g (8 oz) cooked ham, diced
6 tomatoes, skinned, seeded and
  quartered
150ml (5 fl. oz) single cream
2 tbsp chopped parsley
50g (2 oz) butter
freshly ground black pepper

Cook the spaghetti in plenty of fast-boiling salted water for about 12 minutes or until tender. Drain well. Add all the remaining ingredients to the pan and return the spaghetti, heat over a gentle heat tossing lightly with two forks. Taste and check seasoning and serve at once.

Quiches and pizzas

Quiche Lorraine with crisp golden pastry, creamy egg and cheese filling . . . it has come a long way from the old bacon and egg pie. Home made pizza, melt-in-the-mouth flan filled with smoked haddock and tomato, and a very special crab quiche for a lunch or supper party . . . these are dishes to savour and linger over.

For a drinks party, try baby quiches, savoury mouthfuls to be served either hot or cold. Make a batch of pizzas (there's a recipe for a quick scone base if you haven't time enough to make a yeast dough). Eat some with your favourite topping, freeze the rest for later use with different toppings.

The varieties are endless. Flavour with green peppers, tomatoes, spinach and onion, garnish with watercress. Cheese can be Cheddar, Gruyère, Emmenthal, Parmesan. There are no hard-and-fast rules and any well-flavoured cheese will give good results. Essentially, quiches and pizzas should look as good as they taste.

Watercress and Cheddar quiche   *Serves 4–6*

Serve this quiche hot with a tomato salad.

Pastry
175g (6 oz) flour
40g (1½ oz) margarine
40g (1½ oz) lard
6 tsp approx. cold water to mix

Filling
2 eggs, beaten
300ml (10 fl. oz) single cream
salt and pepper
75g (3 oz) full-flavoured Cheddar cheese,
  finely grated
½ bunch watercress, finely chopped
25g (1 oz) butter
1 small onion, finely chopped

To make the pastry, sift the flour into a bowl and add the magarine and lard cut in small pieces and rub in with the fingertips until the mixture resembles fine breadcrumbs. Add just sufficient cold water, about 6 teaspoons to mix to a firm dough. Roll out the pastry fairly thinly and use to line a 22.5cm (9 in.) metal flan dish. Chill in the refrigerator for 15 minutes.

Heat the oven to 220°C (425°F), gas mark 7 and place a baking sheet in it. Line the flan with a piece of greaseproof paper, weigh down with baking beans and then bake blind for 15 minutes.

For the filling, blend the eggs, cream, seasoning, cheese and watercress together in a bowl. Melt the butter in a small pan and gently cook the onion for about 10 minutes or until soft but not brown, and stir into the filling mixture.

Remove the paper and beans from the flan and pour in the filling, return to the oven and reduce the heat to 180°C (350°F), gas mark 4 and bake for 25 to 35 minutes or until the filling is set.

Green pepper and Cheddar quiche   *Serves 4–6*

Make as above but substitute ½ green pepper for the bunch of watercress.

Smoked haddock flan   *Serves 6*

This makes 225g (8 oz) smoked haddock serve six really good portions for supper.

Pastry
175g (6 oz) plain flour
40g (1½ oz) margarine
40g (1½ oz) lard
6 tsp approx. cold water to mix

Filling
25g (1 oz) butter
1 onion, finely sliced
150ml (5 fl. oz) top of the milk
salt and pepper
2 eggs, beaten
3 large tomatoes, skinned and sliced
225g (8 oz) cooked, flaked smoked haddock
50g (2 oz) full-flavoured Cheddar cheese, grated

Make the pastry as for Watercress and Cheddar quiche (page 48) and bake blind for 15 minutes, then remove the baking beans.

Meanwhile make the filling. Melt the butter in a small saucepan and add the onion and cook gently without browning for about 10 minutes, draw off the heat and stir in the milk and season well. Add the beaten eggs.

Arrange the tomato slices in the base of the flan with the smoked haddock on top, season and then pour over the milk mixture. Sprinkle with the cheese and return to the oven, reduce the heat to 180°C (350°F), gas mark 4 and bake the flan for 25 to 35 minutes until the filling is set.

Cheese and spinach quiche   *Serves 6*

A delicious quiche, ideal for a light lunch or supper party.

Pastry

175g (6 oz) plain flour
100g (4 oz) butter
1 egg yolk

40g (1½ oz) Parmesan cheese,
 finely grated
1 tbsp approx. cold water to mix

Filling

450g (1 lb) fresh spinach, cooked
 and drained or 225g (8 oz) packet
 frozen spinach
300ml (10 fl. oz) single cream

salt and pepper
2 eggs
50g (2 oz) full-flavoured Cheddar
 cheese, finely grated

Sift the flour into a bowl, add the butter cut in small pieces and rub in with the fingertips until the mixture resembles fine breadcrumbs, stir in the Parmesan cheese. Blend the water with the egg yolk and add to the flour and mix to a firm dough. Roll out on a lightly floured table fairly thinly and line the flan dish. Chill in the refrigerator for 15 minutes. Heat the oven to 220°C (425°F), gas mark 7 with a baking sheet in it.

Cook the spinach as instructed on the packet and drain thoroughly. Bake the flan blind by lining with a piece of greaseproof paper and weighing down with baking beans for 15 minutes, then remove the paper and beans and spread the spinach over the base of the flan.

Mix together the cream, seasoning and eggs and pour over the spinach. Sprinkle with the Cheddar cheese. Return to the oven, reduce the heat 180°C (350°F), gas mark 4 and bake for a further 25 to 35 minutes or until the filling is set and a pale golden brown.

Quick pizza   *Serves 4*

To save time in making a yeast dough, you can make a scone base and be sure to roll it out fairly thinly.

175g (6 oz) self-raising flour
½ level tsp salt
50g (2 oz) butter
1 egg, beaten
2–3 tbsp milk
1 onion, sliced
4 tomatoes, sliced
salt and pepper
1 level tsp mixed dried herbs
100g (4 oz) Emmenthal cheese, sliced
50g (2 oz) can anchovy fillets, drained

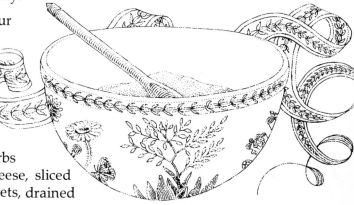

Heat the oven to 220°C (425°F), gas mark 7 and lightly grease a baking sheet.

Place the flour, salt and half the butter in a bowl and rub in with the fingertips until the mixture resembles breadcrumbs and then add the egg and sufficient milk to bind to a firm dough. Knead lightly and then roll out on a floured surface to a circle 6mm (¼ in.) thick and about 20cm (8 in.) in diameter and place on the baking sheet.

Melt the remaining butter in a frying pan and add the onion and fry until soft but not brown for about 5 to 10 minutes, lift out with a slotted spoon and place on the scone base. Slice the tomatoes and arrange on top of the onion, season well and then sprinkle with herbs and finally cover with the slices of cheese.

Decorate with the anchovy fillets in a lattice pattern and bake in the oven for about 30 minutes. Serve hot with a tossed green salad.

Quiche Lorraine *Serves 4–6*

This flan is delicious served straight from the oven or is just as good to take on a picnic.

Pastry
175g (6 oz) plain flour
40g (1½ oz) margarine
40g (1½ oz) lard
6 tsp approx. cold water

Filling
100g (4 oz) Gruyère cheese, sliced
4 rashers streaky bacon
150ml (5 fl. oz) single cream
2 large eggs
1 tsp chopped fresh parsley
1 tsp chopped chives
salt and pepper

Make the pastry as for Watercress and Cheddar quiche (page 48). Heat the oven to 220°C (425°F), gas mark 7 and bake the flan blind for 15 minutes, then remove the baking beans.

Arrange the cheese slices in the bottom of the flan case. Remove the rind from the bacon and fry lightly for 1 to 2 minutes, cut each rasher in half and arrange spoke fashion on top of the cheese. Mix together the cream, eggs, parsley and chives with plenty of seasoning. Pour into the flan case and return to the oven, reduce the heat 180°C (350°F), gas mark 4 and bake for 25 to 35 minutes or until the filling is set.

Baby quiches *Makes 20*

Good to serve with drinks.

Pastry
225g (8 oz) plain flour
½ level tsp salt
50g (2 oz) butter
50g (2 oz) lard
8 tsp approx. cold water

Filling
5 rashers streaky bacon
50g (2 oz) full-flavoured Cheddar cheese, grated
2 eggs, beaten
6 tbsp single cream or top of the milk
1 tsp chopped parsley
salt and pepper

Heat the oven to 190°C (375°F), gas mark 5.

Make the pastry as for Watercress and Cheddar quiche (page 48) and roll out thinly on a floured table and cut out 20 circles with a 7.5cm (3 in.) cutter. Line 20 small bun tins or tart tins with the pastry, prick well and bake blind for 10 minutes.

Meanwhile remove the rind from the bacon and cut into small strips and fry gently for about 2 minutes to let the fat run out, lift out and drain on kitchen paper. Divide with the cheese between the pastry cases. Blend the eggs, cream, parsley and seasoning together and pour into the pastry cases. Return to the oven, reduce the temperature to 160°C (325°F), gas mark 3 and bake for a further 15 to 20 minutes or until the filling is set. Serve either hot or cold.

French onion quiche *Serves 4–6*

Best served warm with a salad and chunks of French bread.

Pastry
175g (6 oz) plain flour   40g (1½ oz) lard
40g (1½ oz) margarine   6 tsp approx. cold water

Filling
40g (1½ oz) butter   salt and pepper
225g (8 oz) onions, finely sliced   75g (3 oz) full-flavoured Cheddar
2 large eggs   cheese, grated
300ml (10 fl. oz) single cream

Make the pastry as for Watercress and Cheddar quiche (page 48). Heat the oven to 220°C (425°F), gas mark 7 and bake the flan blind for 15 minutes, then remove the baking beans.

Meanwhile prepare the filling. Melt the butter in a small pan, add the onion and cook gently for about 10 minutes or until the onions are soft but not brown; place in the flan case. Mix together the eggs, cream and seasoning and pour into the flan case. Sprinkle over the cheese. Return the flan to the oven, reduce the heat to 180°C (350°F), gas mark 4 and bake for 25 to 35 minutes or until the filling is set and a pale golden brown.

Pissaladière *Serves 6*

Since the filling is a rich tomato and onion combination, it is essential to reduce it to evaporate the surplus liquid, otherwise the pastry will go soggy.

Pastry

175g (6 oz) plain flour	1 egg, beaten
75g (3 oz) unsalted butter	1–2 tbsp approx. cold water to mix

Filling

3 tbsp oil	1 rounded tbsp chopped parsley
450g (1 lb) onions, finely sliced	½ level tsp salt
2 cloves garlic, crushed	freshly ground black pepper
400g (14 oz) can tomatoes, roughly chopped	75g (3 oz) full-flavoured Cheddar cheese, grated
1 level tbsp tomato purée	42g (1¾ oz) can anchovies
1 level tsp sugar	12 stuffed green olives

To prepare the pastry, put the flour into a bowl and rub in the butter until the mixture resembles fine breadcrumbs, add the egg and enough cold water to make the pastry come cleanly away from the sides of the bowl. Turn onto a floured table and then knead lightly. Roll out and line a 22.5cm (9 in.) flan ring. Prick the base lightly with a fork and leave to rest for 15 minutes in the refrigerator.

Meanwhile prepare the filling. Heat the oil in a pan and add the onion and garlic, cover and cook over a low heat until soft, stirring occasionally. This will take about 30 minutes. Put the tomatoes in another pan with the purée and sugar and boil rapidly until reduced to about 150ml (5 fl. oz). Stir into the onions with the parsley and seasoning and leave to cool.

Heat the oven to 200°C (400°F), gas mark 6 and then bake the flan blind for 15 minutes (see Watercress and Cheddar quiche, page 48). Then remove from the oven and spoon in the filling. Sprinkle with cheese and arrange the anchovies in a lattice pattern on top, placing an olive in each space. Return to the oven and cook for a further 25 minutes until the cheese is just starting to brown.

Pizzas *Makes 4 pizzas at 3 portions each*

It is a good idea to make lots of pizzas at once. Make one or two to eat now and then put the others in the freezer for another meal. Vary the toppings to suit your fancy.

Base
450ml (15 fl. oz) hand-hot water
1 tsp sugar
12½g (½ oz) dried yeast (3 level tsp)
675g (1½ lb) strong bread flour
3 level tsp salt
12½g (½ oz) lard

Topping 1
400g (14 oz) can tomatoes, drained and roughly chopped
salt and pepper
8 black olives, halved and stoned
50g (2 oz) full-flavoured Cheddar cheese, grated

Topping 2
50g (2 oz) sliced salami
100g (4 oz) mushrooms, sliced
25g (1 oz) butter
75g (3 oz) Emmenthal cheese, sliced
paprika

Topping 3
400g (14 oz) can tomatoes, drained and roughly chopped
¼ tsp oregano
salt and freshly ground black pepper
75g (3 oz) Emmenthal cheese, sliced
anchovy fillets

Topping 4
1 small onion, finely chopped
1 green pepper, pith and seeds removed and diced
1 tbsp oil
100g (4 oz) ham, diced
4 tomatoes, sliced
50g (2 oz) full-flavoured Cheddar cheese, grated

Dissolve the sugar in the water, sprinkle on the yeast and leave for 10 to 15 minutes until frothy.

Put the flour in a large bowl with the salt and rub in the lard; pour on the yeast liquid and mix well to a dough that will leave the sides of the bowl clean. Turn onto a floured table and knead until smooth and no longer sticky, this will take about 10 minutes, or until the dough is smooth and feels firm and elastic. Shape into a large ball, place in a large polyethene bag greased with a little oil and leave in a warm place to rise until double in bulk. Turn the dough out onto a floured table and knead back to the original bulk. Divide the dough into four equal portions and roll each cut to a 20cm (8 in.) circle on a baking sheet and brush each circle with a little oil.

To make topping 1, mix together the tomatoes, seasoning and olives and spread over one of the dough circles and sprinkle with the cheese.

To make topping 2, cover the second circle of dough with the slices of salami. Fry the mushrooms in the butter and spread over the salami. Arrange the cheese slices on top and sprinkle with paprika.

To make topping 3, mix the tomatoes with the oregano and seasoning, spread over the third dough circle. Cover with the cheese slices and arrange the anchovy fillets in a lattice pattern on top.

To make topping 4, fry the onion and green pepper in the oil until the onion is soft. Stir in the ham and spread over the last dough circle and arrange the tomato slices on top. Sprinkle over the cheese.

Heat the oven to 220°C (425°F), gas mark 7. Leave the pizzas in a warm place for about 20 minutes or until the dough is slightly puffy. Bake in the oven for about 20 to 25 minutes until the cheese is golden brown and bubbling and the dough is well risen and crisp. Serve warm.

Pan-fried pizza   *Serves 4*

An easy to make cheese scone-based pizza, topped generously with a tomato, olive and cheese mixture. Essential to cook slowly over a low heat to ensure that the pizza base is cooked thoroughly. Making a pizza this way means a great saving of fuel as it is cooked on the hob, but take care that the underneath of the pizza doesn't burn.

Topping
400g (14 oz) can tomatoes
1 large onion, chopped
1 clove garlic, crushed
½ level tsp mixed dried herbs
salt and pepper
8 stuffed green olives, sliced

Base
175g (6 oz) self-raising flour
½ level tsp baking powder
50g (2 oz) margarine
6–7 tbsp milk
75g (3 oz) Cheddar cheese, grated

Put the contents of the can of tomatoes, onion, garlic, herbs and plenty of seasoning in a small saucepan, bring to the boil and cook quickly for about 5 to 7 minutes or until the sauce has thickened and reduced by half. Remove from the heat, taste and check seasoning and stir in the olives.

To make the pizza base, sift the flour and baking powder into a bowl and rub in the margarine until the mixture resembles fine breadcrumbs. Make a well in the centre and add sufficient milk to make a soft dough. Turn onto a floured board and knead lightly until smooth. Press out into a round, 20cm (8 in.) diameter.

Thoroughly grease a 20cm (8 in.) preferably non-stick frying pan and place the dough in it. Cover and cook very slowly over a low heat until the dough has risen and is puffy and a pale golden brown underneath. This will take about 20 minutes. Spread the tomato mixture on top and sprinkle with cheese then cook under a hot grill for 4 to 5 minutes until the cheese is golden and bubbling. Serve with a green salad.

Crab quiche *Serves 6*

A very special quiche, served either as a first course for a dinner party, when it would serve eight or as an ideal special lunch party. Best served warm.

Pastry
175g (6 oz) plain flour
100g (4 oz) butter
40g (1½ oz) Parmesan cheese, finely grated
1 tbsp approx. cold water to mix
1 egg yolk

Filling
175g (6 oz) crab meat
300ml (10 fl. oz) single cream
salt and pepper
2 eggs
1–2 tbsp finely chopped chives, optional
12½ (½ oz) Parmesan cheese, finely grated

Make the pastry as for Cheese and spinach quiche (see page 50) and roll out on a lightly floured table and line a 22.5cm (9 in.) metal flan dish. Chill in the refrigerator for 15 minutes and then bake blind in a hot oven with a baking sheet in it for 15 minutes at 220°C (425°F), gas mark 7.

Mix together the crab meat, cream, seasoning, eggs and chives. Remove the paper and beans from the flan and pour in the crab mixture, return to the oven and reduce the heat to 180°C (350°F), gas mark 4 and sprinkle the top of the flan with the Parmesan cheese. Bake for a further 25 to 30 minutes or until golden brown and set.

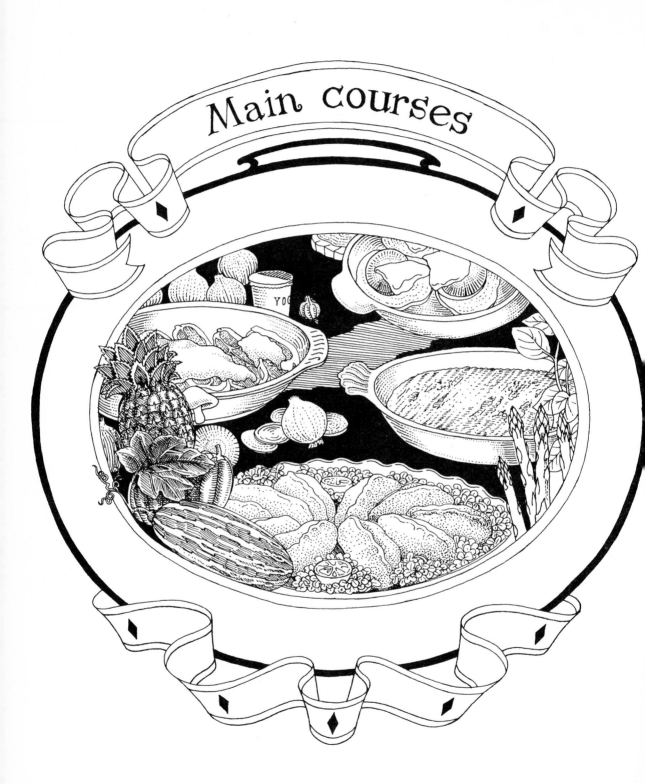

Main courses

It may be Sunday lunch for the family, it may be a good hearty supper after a day out, or the main course of a dinner party. It may feature fish, meat or vegetables, it may be based on the remains of the weekend joint, minced chicken or chopped bacon from the fridge; or it may be centred on a special purchase for a gala dinner – fillet of pork, perhaps, or lamb chops. Whatever the occasion, this is the centre piece of the meal.

You can start a meal with cheese and you can end a meal with cheese. This time, for a change, make cheese part of the main dish. It adds flavour and interest; it can transform vegetables, or do wonders for left-overs; and it brings an extra touch of luxury to a pork chop. It goes without saying that cheese nourishes and enriches.

Scallop pie   *Serves 4*

Scallops are now an expensive item, so it is important to make them go a long way.

450g (1 lb) haddock fillet
4 scallops
450ml (15 fl. oz) milk
1 bayleaf
6 peppercorns
2 sprigs of parsley
¼ level tsp dried dill
40g (1½ oz) butter
40g (1½ oz) flour
675g (1½ lb) potatoes, peeled
100g (4 oz) full-flavoured Cheddar cheese, grated

Put the fish in a pan with the scallops, milk, herbs and a little seasoning. Cover and simmer for 10 to 15 minutes or until the fish flakes easily. Lift the fish from the pan, skin, flake and remove any bones. Quarter the scallops. Save the fish liquor.

Melt the butter in a pan and add the flour and cook for a minute. Strain the fish liquor and stir into pan and bring to the boil, stirring until thickened. Add the flaked fish and scallops and season well. Turn into a 1.7 litre approx. (3 pt) ovenproof dish.

Cook the potatoes and drain well and then mash with a little milk and butter. Stir in 75g (3 oz) cheese and pile on top of the fish. Sprinkle with the remaining cheese and bake in a hot oven 200°C (400°F), gas mark 6 for 30 minutes or until hot through and the cheese has turned golden brown on top.

Monday beef crumble pie   *Serves 4–6*

Make with either marrow or overgrown courgettes in summer. Makes the
last scrappy bits of the Sunday joint go a long way.

25g (1 oz) dripping
1 large onion, chopped
25g (1 oz) flour
300ml (10 fl. oz) water
1 beef stock cube
225g (8 oz) cooked beef, minced
a little gravy browning
½ tsp salt
pepper
450g (1 lb) marrow
225g (8 oz) tomatoes, skinned and
  sliced

Crumble
100g (4 oz) plain flour
50g (2 oz) butter
50g (2 oz) full-flavoured Cheddar
  cheese, finely grated

Heat the oven to 190°C (375°F), gas mark 5.

Heat the dripping in a pan and fry the onion for 5 to 8 minutes or until
golden brown, stir in the flour and cook for 2 minutes until starting to
brown, then add the water and stock cube and bring to the boil, stirring
until thickened. Add the beef, a little gravy browning and salt and pepper
and simmer for 3 minutes.

Peel the marrow, cut in slices and remove all the seeds and then cut in
1.25cm (½ in.) dice and put half in a 1.5 litre (2½ pt) ovenproof dish and
top with half of the minced beef mixture. Repeat the marrow and meat
layers and then arrange the tomato slices on top. To make the crumble, put
the flour in a bowl and rub in the butter until the mixture resembles fine
breadcrumbs, then stir in the cheese. Spoon the crumble mixture onto the
tomatoes and press down lightly and bake in the oven for about 40
minutes or until the crumble has started to turn brown and the marrow is
cooked.

Creamed ham and asparagus   *Serves 4*

A quick supper dish made from ingredients usually found in the store cupboard.

1 small onion, chopped
40g (1½ oz) butter
298g (10½ oz) can condensed cream of chicken or celery soup
3 tbsp dry sherry
225g (8 oz) cooked ham or bacon cut in 1.25cm (½ in.) cubes
340g (12 oz) can asparagus tips, drained
75g (3 oz) full-flavoured Cheddar cheese, grated
175g (6 oz) noodles
1 tbsp freshly chopped parsley
freshly ground black pepper

Heat the oven to 200°C (400°F), gas mark 6.

Fry the onion gently in 12½g (½ oz) of butter until soft, but not brown, this will take about 10 minutes. Stir in the soup and sherry. Put the ham in a shallow 1 litre (2 pt) ovenproof dish and lay the asparagus on top, then pour over the hot soup mixture. Sprinkle with the cheese and bake in the oven for 25 to 30 minutes until hot through and the cheese has melted and is golden brown.

Meanwhile cook the noodles as directed on the packet in boiling salted water. Drain thoroughly and return to the pan with the remaining butter and parsley and toss thoroughly, season well with plenty of freshly ground black pepper and serve with the creamed ham and asparagus.

Plaice Florentine *Serves 4*

Use either plaice fillets or less expensive frozen small cod cutlets.

4 large plaice fillets
salt and ground black pepper
300ml (10 fl. oz) milk
150ml (5 fl. oz) cider
450g (1 lb) fresh spinach, cooked
  and drained or 269g (9½ oz)
  packet frozen leaf spinach
40g (1½ oz) butter
40g (1½ oz) flour
100g (4 oz) full-flavoured Cheddar
  cheese, grated
12½g (½ oz) dried breadcrumbs

Season fillets well with salt and black pepper, fold in three, skin-side innermost, and lay in a shallow pan with the milk and simmer for 10 minutes or until the fish is cooked. Strain the milk into a measure with the cider.

Cook the spinach as directed on the packet and drain thoroughly.

Melt the butter in a small pan and add the flour and cook for a minute, then stir in the milk and cider and bring to the boil, stirring until thickened. Simmer for 2 minutes and season well, add 75g (3 oz) of cheese and stir until melted.

Blend a third of the sauce with the spinach and place in the bottom of a 1 litre (2 pt) ovenproof dish and then arrange the fish on top. Pour over the remaining sauce, mix the remaining cheese with the breadcrumbs and sprinkle on top of the sauce. Place under a hot grill for about 5 minutes or until the top is golden brown and bubbling.

Turkey Milano *Serves 4*

Chicken could equally well be used for this supper dish.

450g (1 lb) French beans, top and tailed
salt
62½g (2½ oz) butter
40g (1½ oz) flour
450ml (15 fl. oz) milk
100g (4 oz) full-flavoured Cheddar cheese, grated
225g (8 oz) cooked diced turkey
ground black pepper
25g (1 oz) fresh white breadcrumbs

Cook the beans in boiling salted water until barely tender, drain well and rinse in cold water and then drain again. Lay the beans in a shallow 1.7 litre (3 pt) ovenproof dish.

Melt 40g (1½ oz) butter in a pan, add the flour and cook for a minute, blend in the milk and bring to the boil, stirring until thickened and then simmer for 2 minutes. Remove from the heat and add the cheese, turkey and seasoning and spoon over the beans.

Melt the remaining butter in a pan and add the breadcrumbs and fry slowly until crisp and brown, then scatter over the turkey mixture. When required reheat in a hot oven 200°C (400°F), gas mark 6 for 20 to 30 minutes or until hot through. Serve with bread rolls or French bread.

Bacon, egg and cheese pie   *Serves 4–6*

This is ideal picnic fare.

Pastry
225g (8 oz) plain flour
50g (2 oz) margarine
50g (2 oz) lard
8 tsp approx. cold water to mix

Filling
100g (4 oz) bacon rashers
75g (3 oz) full-flavoured Cheddar cheese, grated
4–6 eggs
salt and pepper

Make the pastry as for Watercress and Cheddar quiche (page 48) and roll out two thirds and line a 20cm (8 in.) deep metal pie plate.

Chop the bacon rashers and fry lightly to allow the fat to run out, lift out with a slotted spoon and put in the base of the flan, sprinkle with half of the cheese and then carefully break the eggs on top, season well and then sprinkle over the remaining cheese. Damp the edges of the pastry.

Roll out the remaining pastry to form a lid and carefully cover the pie, make a slit in the centre and firmly seal the edges. Brush the top with a little milk. Bake in the oven at 200°C (400°F), gas mark 6 for 25 to 30 minutes or until the pastry is golden brown. Remove from the oven and leave to cool. Serve cut in wedges with a salad.

Muffled chicken *Serves 4*

When the chicken is cut it looks splendid with the bright green stripe of spinach stuffing in the centre.

4 chicken breast portions
50g (2 oz) butter, softened
grated rind of 1 lemon
450g (1 lb) fresh spinach, cooked
    and drained or 225g (8 oz) packet
    frozen leaf spinach, thawed and
    drained thoroughly
salt
plenty of freshly ground black
    pepper
4 slices ham
25g (1 oz) butter
25g (1 oz) flour
300ml (10 fl. oz) milk
75g (3 oz) full-flavoured Cheddar
    cheese, grated

Remove the skin from the chicken, cut off the wing tips and carefully remove the bones. Make a slit half way through the breasts to make a pocket.

Blend the 50g (2 oz) butter with the lemon rind, spinach and salt and black pepper and divide between chicken breasts, packing into the pockets. Wrap each piece of chicken in a slice of ham and place tightly packed in a shallow ovenproof dish.

Heat the oven to 190°C (375°F), gas mark 5.

Melt the remaining butter in a small pan, add the flour and cook for a minute, blend in the milk and bring to the boil, stirring until thickened, then simmer for 2 minutes. Season well and stir in 50g (2 oz) of the cheese and spoon the sauce over the chicken and ham rolls. Sprinkle with the remaining cheese and bake in the oven for about 40 to 45 minutes or until golden brown and bubbling and the chicken is tender.

Eggs Florentine *Serves 2*

A simple dish for supper or when vegetarian friends are visiting serve with slices of hot French bread or crispy rolls.

450g (1 lb) fresh spinach
salt
4 eggs
25g (1 oz) butter
25g (1 oz) flour
300ml (10 fl. oz) milk
pepper
75g (3 oz) full-flavoured
  Cheddar cheese, grated
2 tbsp double cream
1 tbsp grated Parmesan cheese

Heat the oven 180°C (350°F), gas mark 4. Lightly butter a shallow ovenproof dish.

Thoroughly wash the spinach, tear out the stalks and put in a saucepan with some salt, cover with a tightly fitting lid and place over a medium heat to cook for about 10 minutes, stirring occasionally until the spinach is tender. Drain very thoroughly to get rid of all the water and spread in the dish.

Melt the butter in a small pan and add the flour and cook for a minute, stir in the milk and bring to the boil, stirring until the sauce has thickened. Season well and stir in the Cheddar cheese and cream.

Make four dips in the spinach and crack an egg into each. Spoon over the sauce carefully, sprinkle with Parmesan cheese, bake in the oven for about 20 minutes or until the eggs are just set. Serve at once.

Gougère   *Serves 6*

This choux pastry with added cheese is a French recipe and is sometimes baked straight onto a baking sheet with no filling. The French serve it cut in slices whilst still warm or even very thinly sliced as an appetiser with drinks.

Choux pastry
100g (4 oz) butter
300ml (10 fl. oz) water
150g (5 oz) plain flour
4 eggs
½ tsp salt
pepper
1 tsp Dijon mustard
75g (3 oz) Gruyère cheese, diced

Filling
2 onions, sliced
40g (1½ oz) butter
2 level tsp paprika
12½g (½ oz) flour
300ml (10 fl. oz) chicken stock
100g (4 oz) button mushrooms, quartered
170g (6 oz) can red peppers drained and sliced
225g (8 oz) cooked chicken, diced
1 tsp salt
pepper
1 tbsp grated Gruyère cheese

Grease the sides of a 1.7 litre approx. (3 pt) shallow ovenproof dish.

To prepare the choux pastry, place the butter and water in a small pan and bring slowly to the boil, remove from the heat and toss in the flour, quickly and vigorously stir with a wooden spoon to a smooth thick paste which clings to the spoon. Leave to cool slightly.

Meanwhile prepare the filling. Cook the onions in the butter until soft but not browned; this will take about 10 minutes. Add the paprika and flour and cook gently for a minute, stir in the stock and bring to the boil, stirring. Add the mushrooms, peppers, chicken and seasoning and simmer for 5 minutes, then cool.

To complete the choux pastry, whisk the eggs and gradually beat into the cooled paste one spoonful at a time. This may be done with an electric mixer or in a pan with a wooden spoon. When all the egg has been added the mixture will be stiff enough to just hold its shape. Finally beat in the seasoning, mustard and cheese. Spoon around the edge of the dish to form an even border.

Spoon the filling into the centre of the dish, sprinkle with grated Gruyère cheese and bake in a hot oven 200°C (400°F), gas mark 6 for 35 to 45 minutes or until the choux pastry is well risen and golden brown. Serve hot straight from the oven with a green vegetable, e.g. beans or broccoli.

Russian chops   *Serves 4*

An unusual way of serving lamb chops that gives them a delicious flavour.

25g (1 oz) lard
4 loin lamb chops
1 large onion, sliced
4 thin slices full-flavoured Cheddar cheese
150ml (5 fl. oz) yogurt
3 tbsp top milk
salt and freshly ground black pepper
watercress to garnish

Heat the oven to 220°C (425°F), gas mark 7.
   Melt the lard in a frying pan and fry the chops and onion for about 10 minutes, turning the chops once until they are brown on both sides. Lift the chops and onions out of the pan with a slotted spoon and place in a single layer in a shallow ovenproof dish and cover each chop with a slice of cheese. Place in the oven for about 10 minutes or until the cheese has melted.
   Blend the yogurt with the milk and plenty of seasoning and pour over the chops, return to the oven for a further 2 to 3 minutes only. Serve at once garnished with small sprigs of watercress.

Moussaka   *Serves 6–8*

Blanching the aubergines in water is far nicer than the traditional method and not nearly so fatty.

1 small shoulder of lamb minced gives about 550–700g (1¼–1½ lb) meat
225g (8 oz) onions, chopped
2 cloves garlic, crushed
40g (1½ oz) flour
1½ level tsp salt
ground black pepper
1 level tsp coriander seeds, crushed
¼ level tsp dried thyme
400g (14 oz) can tomatoes
4 aubergines

Sauce
40g (1½ oz) butter
40g (1½ oz) flour
450ml (15 fl. oz) milk
1 level tsp made English mustard
grated nutmeg
salt and pepper
175g (6 oz) full-flavoured Cheddar cheese, grated
1 egg, beaten
chopped parsley to garnish

Heat the oven to 190°C (375°F), gas mark 5. Butter a large ovenproof dish 1.7 litre approx. (3 pt) or larger.

Turn the minced lamb into a large pan, cook over a low heat at first to let the fat run out from the meat and stir to prevent sticking. When the fat has run freely from the meat, add the onions and garlic and increase the heat. Fry to brown the meat for about 15 minutes. If there seems to be an excess of fat, spoon off the surplus. Add flour, stir well, then add salt, pepper, coriander, thyme and the can of tomatoes. Bring to the boil and simmer for 5 minutes, taste and check seasoning.

Slice the aubergines into about 6mm (¼ in.) slices and blanch in a pan of boiling water for 1 minute. This softens the skin and prevents the aubergines discolouring. Drain in a colander, then dry on kitchen paper.

Make the sauce by slowly melting the butter in a pan, add the flour and cook for a minute. Blend in the milk, slowly at first, and bring to the boil, stirring well. Add mustard, nutmeg, salt, pepper and cheese. Cook to let the cheese melt, then remove from the heat. Cool slightly and then add the egg, mixing well.

Now assemble the moussaka. First put a layer of half the meat mixture in the dish, cover with half the aubergines, season and then repeat with the rest of the lamb and aubergines, so that you end up with four layers. Pour over the cheese sauce. Bake uncovered for 45 minutes to 1 hour until the moussaka is golden brown. Sprinkle with chopped parsley and serve with hot French bread if liked.

Hereford pork chops   *Serves 4*

Take care to trim excess fat from the chops, otherwise the dish might be greasy.

100g (4 oz) mushrooms, sliced	300ml (10 fl. oz) dry cider
2 cooking apples, peeled, cored and sliced	50g (2 oz) browned breadcrumbs
	50g (2 oz) full-flavoured Cheddar cheese, grated
1 onion, sliced	
salt and pepper	watercress or parsley to garnish
4 pork chops	

Heat the oven to 200°C (400°F), gas mark 6 and lightly grease a shallow 1.7 litre approx. (3 pt) ovenproof dish. Place the mushrooms, cooking apples and onions in the base of the dish and season well. Trim the rind and any excess fat from the chops and lay on the bed of vegetables and pour over the cider.

Mix together the browned breadcrumbs and cheese and pile on top of the chops. Bake for 45 to 60 minutes or until the chops are tender and the topping golden brown and crisp. Garnish the dish with sprigs of watercress or parsley and serve.

Quick and easy oven bake   *Serves 4*

A good store-cupboard idea.

2 tomatoes, sliced	298g (10½ oz) can condensed mushroom soup
100g (4 oz) cooked peas	
198g (7 oz) can tuna fish, drained and flaked	3 tbsp milk
	25g (1 oz) packet potato crisps
salt and pepper	50g (2 oz) Cheddar cheese, grated

Heat the oven to 190°C (375°F), gas mark 5.

Place the tomatoes, peas and tuna fish in the bottom of a 1 litre (1½ pt) ovenproof pie dish and season well. Blend the soup with the milk and pour over the tuna fish. Lightly crush the crisps and mix evenly with the cheese, then sprinkle over the top of the soup. Place in the oven and bake for 25 minutes until golden brown and hot through.

Somerset layer   *Serves 4*

An ideal dish for high tea or children's lunch and takes only 10 minutes to put together. If your children dislike herbs leave them out.

450g (1 lb) pork or beef sausagemeat
½ level tsp mixed dried herbs
50g (2 oz) streaky bacon
2 tomatoes, peeled and sliced
salt and pepper
1 large cooking apple, peeled, cored and sliced
100g (4 oz) full-flavoured Cheddar cheese, grated
450g (1 lb) mashed potato or 1 large (4 portion) packet instant

Heat the oven to 180°C (350°F), gas mark 4.

Line the bottom of a 1.7 litre approx. (3 pt) shallow ovenproof dish with the sausagemeat and sprinkle with herbs.

Remove the rind and bone from the bacon and cut in small strips and then gently fry in its own fat for 3 to 4 minutes until the fat has run out, drain and spread over the sausagemeat. Cover with the tomato slices and season well then arrange the apple slices on top and sprinkle with the cheese.

Make up the mashed potato as directed on the packet and spread over the top of the dish. Bake in the oven for 45 to 60 minutes or until the potato is golden brown and the meat cooked through.

Tahiti ham   *Serves 4*

Serve with noodles tossed in melted butter and with a little very finely chopped green pepper added.

4 ham steaks
4 rings pineapple
4 slices full-flavoured Cheddar cheese
12½g (½ oz) butter
12½g (½ oz) flour
150ml (5 fl. oz) milk
1 level tsp made mustard
salt and pepper
2 tbsp vinegar

Heat the grill and then grill the ham steaks for about 5 minutes on each side and lift out and place on a flat ovenproof dish. Place a ring of pineapple on each slice of ham and cover with a slice of cheese. Then return to the grill and allow the cheese to melt.

To make the sauce melt the butter in a small pan and stir in the flour and cook for a minute, then blend in the milk and bring to the boil, stirring until thickened, add the remaining ingredients and simmer gently for 2 minutes. Spoon the sauce over the ham and serve at once.

Foil-baked mackerel   *Serves 4*

These mackerel could also be cooked on a barbecue over a medium heat and then served straight from the parcels with the juice poured over.

4 medium mackerel
50g (2 oz) butter
1 small onion, finely chopped
100g (4 oz) mushrooms, chopped
50g (2 oz) fresh white breadcrumbs
75g (3 oz) full-flavoured Cheddar
   cheese, grated
salt and pepper
lemon slices and parsley to garnish

Heat the oven to 180°C (350°F), gas mark 4. Lightly butter four squares of foil large enough to wrap the mackerel in.

Clean the mackerel and remove the heads and place each fish on a piece of foil, after wiping dry with kitchen paper.

Melt the butter in a saucepan and add the onion and cook gently for 5 minutes, stir in the mushrooms, breadcrumbs and cheese and season well. Use to stuff the mackerel, then close the foil at the sides and ends to seal in the juices. Bake in the oven for about 25 minutes; if liked the foil may be opened for the last 5 minutes of the cooking time. The fish is done when the flesh has turned white and opaque. Garnish with lemon slices and sprigs of parsley and serve hot.

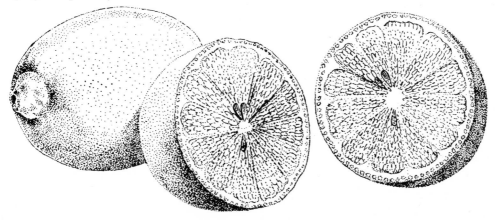

Savoury roly-poly *Serves 4–6*

A filling winter dish with an excellent flavour that all the family will love. For a change add ½ level teaspoon mixed dried herbs to the pastry.

225g (8 oz) self-raising flour
a good pinch salt
100g (4 oz) shredded suet
7–8 tbsp approx. milk
227g (8 oz) can peeled tomatoes
2 onions, finely chopped
100–175g (4–6 oz) full-flavoured Cheddar cheese, grated
beaten egg or milk to glaze

Heat the oven to 200°C (400°F), gas mark 6.

Place the flour and salt in a bowl with the suet and mix well, then add sufficient milk to mix to a soft but not sticky dough and then knead lightly. Roll out on a floured surface to approximately 37.5 × 30cm (15 × 12 in.).

Drain the tomatoes and then place in a bowl and mash lightly, stir in the onion and if the mixture seems a little dry stir in a tablespoon or two of the tomato juice, season very well. Spread over the pastry, leaving a border of 1.25cm (½ in.) around each edge of the pastry and then sprinkle with the cheese. Brush the edge of the pastry with beaten egg or milk and roll up from the long side, Swiss roll fashion, and secure the edges well. Place on a baking sheet and brush all over with beaten egg or milk. Bake for 35 to 40 minutes or until golden brown and serve hot, cut in thick slices.

Haddock mornay *Serves 4*

Serve with buttered leaf spinach and creamy potatoes.

450g (1 lb) tail piece of cod or haddock
2 level tsp chopped fresh mixed herbs
1 level tbsp chopped chives
1 small tomato
salt and pepper
butter
Sauce
25g (1 oz) butter
25g (1 oz) flour
300ml (10 fl. oz) milk
75g (3 oz) full-flavoured Cheddar cheese, grated
1 rounded tsp made English mustard
salt and pepper

Heat the oven to 180°C (350°F), gas mark 4 and butter a shallow ovenproof dish.

Make eight deep slits in the fish, right down to the bone, four on each side. Blend the herbs with the chives and pack the mixture into the slits. Cut the tomato into eight wedges and press into the top of each slit. Place the fish into the dish, season well and dot with a little butter, cover with a piece of buttered paper or foil and bake in the oven for 30 minutes, then remove the cover and bake for a further 10 minutes or until the fish is cooked, the time varying with the thickness of the tail.

Meanwhile prepare the sauce. Melt the butter in a small saucepan and stir in the flour and cook for a minute, then blend in the milk and bring to the boil, stirring until thickened, then simmer for 2 minutes. Add the cheese with the mustard and seasoning, and stir well to allow the cheese to melt. Add any juice from the fish to sauce and serve either separately or if liked it may be spooned over fish.

Saturday bacon bake   *Serves 6*

Especially popular in our house because you can make it the day before and bake it on Saturday. Made from ingredients which you are very likely to have in the 'fridge such as the last cuts of bacon joint, cold left-over potatoes, a few mushrooms and a lump of cheese.

450g (1 lb) potatoes
450g (1 lb) cooked ham or bacon
50g (2 oz) butter
50g (2 oz) flour
600ml (1 pt) milk
175g (6 oz) mushrooms, sliced
3 hard-boiled eggs, roughly chopped
salt and pepper
50g (2 oz) full-flavoured Cheddar cheese, grated
25g (1 oz) Parmesan cheese, grated

Boil the potatoes in their skins until cooked, drain, peel and slice. Cut the ham or bacon into neat cubes.

Melt the butter in a large saucepan, add the flour and cook for 2 minutes. Stir in the milk and bring to the boil, stirring until thickened, then add the mushrooms and simmer for 5 minutes. Add the ham or bacon, potato and eggs, mix well and season to taste.

Turn into a 2 litre (3½ pt) ovenproof dish and sprinkle with cheese, place under a medium grill until brown and hot through. If the pie has been made in advance, bake in an oven at 190°C (375°F), gas mark 5 for about 30 minutes. Serve with French bread and a green salad.

Savoury pancakes *Serves 4*

For a simple meal, prepare these in advance and then put in the oven for about 30 minutes to re-heat. Serve with a green vegetable.

Filling

2 rashers streaky bacon, chopped	150ml (5 fl. oz) stock
450g (1 lb) minced beef	2 level tbsp tomato purée
1 onion, chopped	1 level tsp salt
1 stick celery, chopped	black pepper
12½g (½ oz) flour	a little thyme

Pancakes

100g (4 oz) plain flour	300ml (10 fl. oz) milk and water
¼ tsp salt	mixed
1 egg, beaten	1 tbsp salad oil

Sauce

25g (1 oz) butter	1 level tsp made English mustard
25g (1 oz) flour	salt and pepper
300ml (10 fl. oz) milk	100g (4 oz) full-flavoured Cheddar cheese, grated

To prepare the meat filling, put the bacon, beef, onion and celery in a pan and cook gently for 5 to 10 minutes to allow the fat to run out. Stir in the flour, then add the stock and bring to the boil, stirring. Add the remaining ingredients, cover and simmer for 30 to 40 minutes or until meat is tender.

Meanwhile make the pancakes. Put the flour and salt into a bowl and make a well in the centre. Add the egg and gradually stir in half the milk, using a whisk blend in the flour from the sides of the bowl. Beat well until the mixture is smooth. Stir in the remaining milk and salad oil.

Heat a little oil in a 20cm (8 in.) frying pan. When it is hot pour off any excess oil and spoon about 2 tablespoons of the batter into the pan. Tip and rotate the pan so that the batter spreads out, and thinly covers the bottom of the pan. Cook the pancake for about 1 minute until pale brown underneath, then turn it over with a palette knife and cook for a further minute, turn onto a plate and make more pancakes in the same way. Spread the pancakes on a flat surface and divide the meat mixture between them and roll up and lay in a single layer a shallow ovenproof dish and keep warm

Now prepare the sauce. Melt the butter in a small saucepan, stir in the flour and cook for one minute. Blend in the milk and bring to the boil, stirring until thickened and simmer for 2 minutes. Add 75g (3 oz) of cheese to the sauce with the mustard and seasoning, stir until the cheese has melted. Spoon over the pancakes and sprinkle with the remaining cheese. Place under a moderate grill until the top is golden brown and bubbling. Serve at once.

Chicken and cheese croquettes *Serves 4*

Any left-over cooked chicken or turkey can be used to make these croquettes.

225–275g (8–10 oz) cooked chicken
1 small onion, minced
25g (1 oz) butter
25g (1 oz) flour
150ml (5 fl. oz) chicken stock
salt and pepper

50g (2 oz) full-flavoured Cheddar
 cheese, grated
1 egg, beaten
brown breadcrumbs
fat or oil for deep frying

Remove any skin and hard pieces from the chicken, mince and put on one side. Then mince the onion.

Melt the butter in a saucepan and add the onion, cover and cook gently for about 5 to 8 minutes or until the onion is soft but not brown. Stir in the flour and cook for a minute, stir in the stock and bring to the boil stirring until thickened, then season well and add the cheese. Remove from the heat and beat well, add the minced chicken and mix well. Leave on one side until cold.

Take tablespoonfuls of the mixture and with wetted hands shape into croquettes and then dip in the beaten egg and browned breadcrumbs and pat well to coat thoroughly. Put on a plate and leave in a cool place until required or leave until quite firm before frying. Deep fry in fat or oil for about 5 minutes or until golden brown all over. Lift out and drain on kitchen paper, then serve.

Cheesey cod grill *Serves 4*

The cheese topping gives cod steaks a lift and is so easy to do.

Butter
4 cod steaks or cutlets
salt and pepper
2 tomatoes, halved

100g (4 oz) full-flavoured Cheddar cheese, grated
2 tsp lemon juice
2 level tsp made mustard
parsley to garnish

Heat the grill to moderate and butter a shallow ovenproof dish. Lay in the cod steaks in a single layer and season well and place the tomatoes around. Dot the fish and tomatoes with a little butter and cook under the grill for about 10 minutes, turning once.

Meanwhile blend the cheese with the lemon juice and mustard and then spread over the top of the hot fish, return to the grill and continue cooking for a further 5 minutes or until the cheese has melted and is golden brown and bubbling. Garnish with a sprig of parsley and serve with new potatoes and green peas.

Pork in Parmesan cream sauce *Serves 4*

A dish to serve on a rather special occasion. Broccoli goes very well with it or any crisp green vegetable and sauté potatoes.

4 pork chops
salt and pepper
50g (2 oz) butter

Sauce
25g (1 oz) butter
25g (1 oz) flour
300ml (10 fl. oz) milk
25g (1 oz) grated Parmesan cheese
2 egg yolks
150ml (5 fl. oz) double cream
a little extra Parmesan cheese, grated

Trim the rind and any excess fat from the pork chops and season well. Melt the butter in a large frying pan and fry the chops over a gentle heat for 20 to 25 minutes, turning once until golden brown on both sides.

Meanwhile prepare the sauce. Melt the butter in a small saucepan and stir in the flour and cook for a minute. Blend in the milk and bring to the boil, stirring until thickened and simmer for 2 minutes. Season well and stir in the cheese.

Lift the pork chops out of the frying pan and arrange on an ovenproof serving dish.

Blend the egg yolks with the cream. Draw the sauce from the heat and stir in the egg and cream mixture, blend well and then re-heat for a minute. Spoon over the pork chops and sprinkle the top with a little extra Parmesan cheese and put under a hot grill until golden brown.

Fillet of pork en croûte *Serves 6*

A dinner party special. Easy to serve – no portioning or carving needed.

Pastry
225g (8 oz) strong plain flour
½ tsp salt
25g (1 oz) Parmesan cheese, grated
175g (6 oz) hard margarine

9 tbsp approx. or a scant 150ml
  (5 fl. oz) cold water
a little beaten egg to glaze

Filling
50g (2 oz) butter
675g (1½ lb) pork fillet cut in six
  even sized pieces
1 large onion, chopped

225g (8 oz) mushrooms, sliced
4 tbsp sherry
¼ level tsp mixed dried herbs
salt and pepper

To make the pastry, put the flour and salt into a bowl with the cheese. Coarsely grate the margarine into the bowl and stir in just sufficient water to make a firm dough. Roll out on a lightly floured surface to make a strip about 1.25cm (½ in.) thick and 15cm (6 in.) wide. Fold the pastry in three and give it a quarter turn to the left. Roll out again into a strip and fold in three. Wrap the pastry in foil and chill in the refrigerator until required.

Now prepare the filling. Melt the butter in a frying pan and fry the pork over a medium heat for 15 minutes, turning frequently until golden brown. Lift out with a slotted spoon and put on a plate. Add the onion, mushrooms, sherry, herbs and seasoning to the pan, cover and cook for 15 minutes on a gentle heat until the onion is tender. Lift out and place in a bowl and leave to cool. Heat the oven to 220°C (425°F), gas mark 7.

Roll out the pastry on a lightly floured surface to an oblong 45 × 30cm (18 × 12 in.) and cut into six squares. Divide the meat and mushroom mixture between the squares of pastry. Brush the edges with a little beaten egg and make a neat parcel with the pastry to seal in the filling. Place on the baking tray and brush with more beaten egg and bake for 25 minutes or until golden brown. Serve with a little onion gravy.

Mince carbonnade *Serves 4*

The use of beer in this recipe gives the mince a lovely flavour.

12½g (½ oz) dripping
1 large onion, finely chopped
450g (1 lb) raw minced beef
25g (1 oz) flour
300ml (10 fl. oz) beer
100g (4 oz) button mushrooms
1 level tbsp tomato purée
1 tsp Worcestershire sauce
salt and pepper
350g (12 oz) small new potatoes, cooked
50g (2 oz) full-flavoured Cheddar cheese, grated
1 level tbsp chopped parsley

Melt the dripping in a frying pan and fry the onion and mince for 5 minutes to lightly brown, then stir in the flour and cook for a minute. Add the beer and bring to the boil, stirring; add the mushrooms, tomato purée, Worcestershire sauce and plenty of seasoning. Partially cover the pan with a lid and then simmer for 30 minutes. Add the potatoes and cook for a further 15 minutes. Taste and check seasoning; turn into a hot serving dish.

Mix the cheese and parsley together and then sprinkle over the top of the meat. Serve with a green salad or vegetable.

Cauliflower cheese (have you tried it with bacon and mushrooms?) is everyone's idea of cheese served with a vegetable. But there are lots of other ways, in fact – the possibilities are endless. There are very few vegetables that do not take kindly to the addition of cheese; simply grated over hot cooked vegetables it makes them immediately interesting.

Use it to stuff marrows, aubergines, courgettes. Make it into a creamy sauce for leeks, add it as a crisp topping to chicory baked in the oven. Diced, it is a welcome addition to salads. In salads for slimmers – and others – and in vegetarian recipes, cheese brings that extra nourishment that turns a simple dish into a meal. Try combining hard cheese with raw fruit and vegetables for a salad that is deliciously different – or try cottage cheese which is lighter.

Potatoes take particularly kindly to it. What child does not love a baked potato? Add a cheese topping – there are plenty of varieties – and the grown-ups will go for it too. By using different cheeses and a selection of the ingredients in your store cupboard you can be adventurous and you will find your experiments quickly adopted as family favourites.

Baked aubergines with tomatoes and cheese *Serves 6*

Soft over-ripe tomatoes are fine for this dish, if they are not in season you can use drained canned tomatoes.

1 large onion, chopped
8 tbsp approx. salad oil
2 cloves garlic, crushed
450g (1 lb) tomatoes, skinned and quartered
salt
ground black pepper
175g (6 oz) full-flavoured Cheddar cheese, grated
2 aubergines, sliced

Heat the oven to 200°C (400°F), gas mark 6.

Fry the onion in 2 tablespoons of the oil until soft – this will take about 10 minutes – then add the garlic, stir well and then lift out with a slotted spoon and place in a shallow ovenproof dish with the tomato wedges and season well. Sprinkle over half the grated cheese.

Fry the slices of aubergine in the remaining oil until pale golden brown on both sides and then lift out with a slotted spoon and drain thoroughly on kitchen paper. Place in the dish on top of the tomatoes and onions and cheese. Season well and then scatter over the remaining cheese. Bake in the oven for 30 minutes or until the cheese is beginning to brown.

Cauliflower cheese   *Serves 4*

Adding bacon rolls makes the cauliflower cheese a light main meal.

1 large cauliflower
salt
50g (2 oz) butter
40g (1½ oz) flour
300ml (10 fl. oz) milk
100g (4 oz) full-flavoured Cheddar
  cheese, grated
ground black pepper
½ tsp English made mustard
4 streaky bacon rashers
4 large mushrooms

Divide the cauliflower into large sprigs, and discard any leaves and trim off any thick piece of stem, wash and then cook in boiling salted water for about 5 minutes or until it still has a bone in the stalk. Drain well and reserve 150ml (5 fl. oz) of the cooking liquor.

Melt 40g (1½ oz) butter in a small pan and stir in the flour and cook for a minute. Blend in the milk and bring to the boil, stirring until thickened, and add the reserved cooking liquor. Add 75g (3 oz) of the cheese with the pepper and mustard, stir well so that the cheese melts.

Put the cauliflower in a shallow 1 litre (1½ pt) ovenproof dish and pour over the sauce and scatter the remaining cheese on top. Keep warm.

Stretch the bacon rashers on a wooden board with the back of a knife and cut each in two, then roll up and put on thin skewers and put on a rack in a grill pan. Put the mushrooms stalks upwards alongside and dot with the remaining butter and grill under a hot grill for about 5 minutes, turning the bacon rolls once, then remove from the grill and keep hot.

Put the cauliflower under the grill and grill until the cheese on top is golden brown and bubbling. Garnish with mushrooms and the bacon rolls removed from the skewers and serve with warm bread rolls.

Farmer's potato and bacon pie   *Serves 4*

A good family pie for the end of the week when the housekeeping is low.

900g (2 lb) potatoes	100–175g (4–6 oz) full-flavoured
25g (1 oz) butter	Cheddar cheese, grated
milk	225g (8 oz) bacon pieces
salt and pepper	6–8 spring onions, chopped

Heat the oven to 200°C (400°F), gas mark 6.

Boil the potatoes and mash with the butter, milk and seasoning and beat in three quarters of the cheese.

Put the bacon pieces in a pan and fry gently to let the fat run out, then add the onions and fry quickly for 3 to 4 minutes or until the bacon is crisp and lightly browned.

Spread one third of the potato in a buttered shallow 1 litre (2 pt) ovenproof dish and top with half the bacon and onion mixture. Repeat with potato and bacon layers and then spread the remaining potato on top and sprinkle with the rest of the cheese. Bake in the oven for 15 minutes or until the cheese is golden brown on top. Serve with baked beans.

Welsh leek tart   *Serves 4–6*

Serve after a good home-made soup for an informal supper.

200g (7 oz) frozen packet
  shortcrust pastry, thawed or
  home-made (see page 48)
2 medium leeks
25g (1 oz) butter

Sauce
25g (1 oz) butter
25g (1 oz) flour
300ml (10 fl. oz) milk
75g (3 oz) full-flavoured Cheddar
  cheese, grated
salt and pepper
½ level tsp made English mustard
6 slices streaky bacon, grilled

Heat the oven to 200°C (400°F), gas mark 6.

Roll out the pastry on a floured table and line 17.5cm approx. (7 in.) flan dish, prick the base and line with greaseproof paper and baking beans and bake in the oven for 15 minutes. Remove the greaseproof paper and beans and return the flan to the oven and bake for a further 5 to 10 minutes to dry out the pastry.

Meanwhile wash the leeks thoroughly, then drain well and slice. Heat the butter in a small pan, add the leeks and cover and simmer gently for about 10 minutes or until the leeks are soft.

Now prepare the sauce. Melt the butter in a small pan and stir in the flour and cook for a minute, add the milk and bring to the boil, stirring until thickened and then simmer for 2 minutes, remove from the heat and beat in the cheese, seasoning and mustard and then stir in the leeks. Pour the mixture into the flan case and arrange slices of grilled bacon on top. Serve at once.

Crispy courgettes   *Serves 4*

Courgettes cooked like this make an ideal accompaniment to fish or chicken.

450g (1 lb) medium-sized courgettes
2 eggs approx.
salt and pepper
75–100g (3–4 oz) approx. fresh white breadcrumbs
oil for frying
50g (2 oz) full-flavoured Cheddar cheese, finely grated
paprika

Wipe the courgettes and trim both ends and then cut into slices 0.6cm (¼ in.) thick. Lightly beat the eggs and season well, coat the courgettes in the egg and the breadcrumbs.

Heat the oil in a frying pan and fry the courgettes in a single layer over a moderate heat for 4 to 5 minutes or until golden brown and crisp on the outside and the centre is tender, repeat with the remaining courgettes. Lift out with a slotted spoon and drain on kitchen paper. Pile into a warm serving dish and cover at once with the grated cheese, so that it will start to melt on the hot courgettes.

Sprinkle with a little paprika and serve at once.

Oven-baked potatoes   *Serves 4*

Serve for children's high tea on a cold day with a colourful soup.

4 large potatoes
cooking oil
25–50g (1–2 oz) butter

Scrub the potatoes thoroughly, brush with a little oil and place on a baking tray and bake in a hot oven at 200°C (400°F), gas mark 6 for about 1¼ to 1½ hours depending on the size of the potatoes. If soft-skinned potatoes are preferred they may be rubbed with a little salt and then wrapped in foil and baked for about an hour; again the time will vary slightly with the size of the potato.

Cut each potato in half and then fork up the inside slightly and serve dotted with butter.

Soured cream topping

Scoop out the insides of 4 potatoes into a bowl and add a carton of 150ml (5 fl. oz) soured cream, 50g (2 oz) softened cream cheese and a tablespoon finely chopped chives and mix all together, return to the potato cases and re-heat in the hot oven for about 10 minutes.

Gouda topping

Scoop out the insides of 4 potatoes into a bowl and add 50g (2 oz) finely grated Gouda cheese, 50g (2 oz) finely chopped ham and a level teaspoon of made mustard. Season to taste and return to the potato skins and re-heat in the hot oven for about 10 minutes.

Bacon and cheese topping

De-rind and chop 4 rashers streaky bacon and fry until crisp, turn into a bowl with the scooped-out insides of 4 potatoes, add 50–75g (2–3 oz) finely grated Double Gloucester cheese and mix and season well, then pile back into the potato skins and place a slice of tomato on top of each potato and re-heat in the oven for about 10 minutes.

Cheese and chutney with sausages

Scoop out the insides of 4 potatoes into a bowl and add 50g (2 oz) full-flavoured Cheddar cheese, finely grated and a tablespoon chutney, mix well and pile back into the skins and place a cooked chipolata sausage on top of each potato and re-heat for 10 minutes.

Cream cheese and garlic

Blend together 75g (3 oz) cream cheese and a crushed clove of garlic and 2 tablespoons single cream or top milk and add to the scooped-out insides of 4 potatoes, mix and season well, return to the potato cases and re-heat.

Baked chicory with crisp cheese topping   *Serves 4*

This goes well with something like boiled bacon or bacon chops.

40g (1½ oz) butter
8 small heads chicory, quartered lengthwise
juice of 1 lemon
2 level tsp caster sugar
¼ level tsp salt
freshly ground black pepper
50g (2 oz) mild-flavoured Cheshire cheese, finely grated
50g (2 oz) fresh white breadcrumbs

Heat the oven to 200°C (400°F), gas mark 6 and grease a shallow ovenproof casserole or dish with a little of the butter. Lay in the chicory in a single layer and then dot with the remaining butter; add lemon juice, sugar and seasoning. Cover with a tight-fitting lid or a piece of foil and bake in the oven for 20 to 25 minutes, basting once or twice during cooking until the chicory is tender.

   Mix the cheese with the breadcrumbs, remove the lid from the dish and sprinkle the cheese and crumbs on top of the chicory, return to the oven uncovered for a further 15 minutes or until the top is crispy and golden brown.

Cottage potatoes   *Serves 4*

Cook below the roast on Sunday for a change. These potatoes are especially nice with lamb or roast chicken.

450g (1 lb) potatoes, peeled
100g (4 oz) cottage cheese
1 clove garlic, crushed
1 egg, beaten
450ml (15 fl. oz) milk
salt
freshly ground black pepper
25g (1 oz) butter

Heat the oven to 180°C (350°F), gas mark 4.
   Cut the potatoes into slices and place in a 1.5 litre (2½ pt) ovenproof deep dish.
   Mix together the cheese, garlic, egg, milk and seasoning and pour over the potatoes and then dot with butter. Cover with a lid of foil and cook for 1 hour and then remove the lid and cook for a further 30 minutes or until the potatoes are quite tender when prodded with a knife.

Stuffed green peppers *Serves 4*

This is an ideal supper or lunch dish served with warm bread rolls or chunks of French bread.

75g (3 oz) long grain rice
25g (1 oz) butter
1 small onion, chopped
100g (4 oz) button mushrooms, chopped
2 chicken livers, chopped
salt and ground black pepper
1 rounded tsp chopped parsley
1 egg, beaten
4 large even-sized green peppers

Sauce
25g (1 oz) butter
25g (1 oz) flour
300ml (10 fl. oz) milk
1 level tsp made English mustard
a little salt and pepper
100g (4 oz) full-flavoured Cheddar cheese, grated

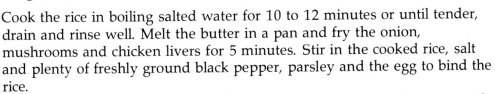

Cook the rice in boiling salted water for 10 to 12 minutes or until tender, drain and rinse well. Melt the butter in a pan and fry the onion, mushrooms and chicken livers for 5 minutes. Stir in the cooked rice, salt and plenty of freshly ground black pepper, parsley and the egg to bind the rice.

Cut a circle from the base of each green pepper to remove the stem and seeds. Arrange the peppers fairly close together in an ovenproof dish and spoon in the filling. Heat the oven to 180°C (350°F), gas mark 4.

To make the sauce, melt the butter in a small pan and add the flour and cook for a minute. Add the milk and bring to the boil, stirring, simmer until thickened, add mustard and seasoning and stir in 50g (2 oz) of the cheese and pour this sauce around the peppers. Sprinkle the top of the peppers with the remaining cheese. Bake in the oven for 45 to 50 minutes or until the peppers are tender.

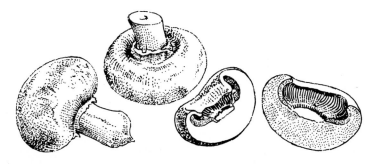

Curried salad eggs   *Serves 4*

Make ahead and then chill before serving.

8 hard-boiled eggs
75g (3 oz) rich cream cheese
1 level tsp curry powder
1 tbsp mango chutney juice
1 rounded tbsp mayonnaise

Rice salad
100g (4 oz) patna rice
2 tomatoes, skinned, seeded
  and chopped
¼ cucumber, peeled and diced
4 spring onions, chopped
3 tbsp French dressing
seasoning to taste
small sprigs of watercress to garnish

Shell the eggs, then cut them in half lengthwise and scoop out the yolks into a bowl, add the cheese, curry powder, mango chutney juice and mayonnaise and mix well with a fork until blended. Spoon the mixture back into the eggs and press halves back together to reshape into whole eggs and put in a cool place to chill.

Cook the rice in fast-boiling salted water until tender and then rinse and drain well. Place in a bowl with the tomatoes, cucumber, spring onions and French dressing and mix well and if necessary add a little seasoning, then cover and put in a cool place. Leave to become quite cold and allow the flavours to blend.

To serve, arrange the rice salad down the centre of a serving dish and place the eggs around the edge and garnish the dish with small sprigs of watercress.

Molly's mushroomburgers   *Serves 3–4*

A really delicious recipe given to me by a vegetarian friend. Put the burgers on the table and watch the plate empty.

100g (4 oz) chopped mushrooms
100g (4 oz) full-flavoured Cheddar cheese, grated
100g (4 oz) wholemeal or brown breadcrumbs
100g (4 oz) finely grated onion
1 level tbsp chopped fresh herbs or parsley

salt and pepper
1 large egg, beaten
a little wholemeal flour
margarine

Put the mushrooms, cheese, breadcrumbs, onion, herbs, seasoning and beaten egg in a bowl and mix thoroughly. Divide the mixture into eight equal portions and shape into burgers and then lightly coat in flour.

Heat the margarine in a frying pan and fry over a moderate heat for 15 to 20 minutes, turning once until golden brown on both sides. Serve hot with potatoes and a green vegetable for a main meal or with fried eggs as a snack.

Baked leeks mornay   *Serves 4*

For a change try substituting celery hearts for the leeks. Serve for supper with chunks of French bread.

4 medium leeks
4 slices ham
25g (1 oz) butter
25g (1 oz) flour
300ml (10 fl. oz) milk
75g (3 oz) full-flavoured Cheddar
  cheese, grated
1 rounded tsp made English
  mustard
salt and pepper
parsley to garnish

Heat the oven to 180°C (350°F), gas mark 4.

Cut the coarse green leaves off the leeks and make a slit through all the green and half the white part of the leeks and open up, keeping the green end down, hold under cold running water to wash very thoroughly, then drain and pat dry on kitchen paper. Wrap each leek in a slice of ham and lay side by side in a shallow ovenproof dish.

Melt the butter in a small saucepan and stir in the flour and cook for a minute, remove from the heat and blend in the milk. Return to the heat and bring to the boil, stirring until thickened and simmer for 2 minutes. Add 50g (2 oz) of the cheese with the mustard and seasoning, stir well to mix and allow the cheese to melt, then spoon over the leeks. Sprinkle with the remaining cheese. Bake in the oven for about 1 hour until the leeks are tender when pierced in the thickest part with a skewer. Garnish with parsley and serve.

Oven-fried potato galette   *Serves 4*

A galette is a large pancake, normally served in France. A large packet of instant mashed potatoes may be used in this recipe in order to save time.

675 (1½ lb) potatoes, peeled
salt
50g (2 oz) butter
2 tbsp milk
175g (6 oz) full-flavoured Cheddar cheese, grated
2 onions, finely chopped
1 egg, beaten
pepper
3 tomatoes
100g (4 oz) streaky bacon, chopped

Cook the potatoes in boiling salted water until soft, then drain well and mash and then beat in the butter and milk with 100g (4 oz) of grated cheese, the chopped onion and beaten egg. Then add pepper and if necessary add a little extra salt.

   Heat the oven to 200°C (400°F), gas mark 6, and butter a shallow 22.5cm approx. (9 in.) ovenproof plate and then press on the potato mixture, smoothing the top flat. Top the potato cake with the slices of tomato in a single layer and then sprinkle with the chopped bacon and finally the remaining cheese. Bake in the oven for about 20 to 25 minutes or until the cheese has melted and is a pale golden brown. Serve hot.

Chicken and cheese mayonnaise   *Serves 4–6*

This is a good way of serving any left-over cold chicken and at Christmas you could use turkey. It makes a delicious cold supper dish when friends call.

225–350g (8–12 oz) cooked diced chicken
2 sticks celery, finely sliced
2 sprigs onions, finely chopped
150–300ml (5–10 fl. oz) mayonnaise, home-made (see page 92) or a good
   bought variety
100g (4 oz) Edam cheese, diced
50g (2 oz) flaked almonds, browned
2 tsp lemon juice
salt and pepper
lettuce
tomatoes

Place the chicken in a large bowl and add the celery, spring onions, mayonnaise, cheese, almonds and lemon juice and mix all together until well blended. Taste and then add seasoning. Cover the bowl and place in the refrigerator for at least an hour for the flavours to blend.

Arrange a bed of lettuce on a flat serving dish and spoon the salad on top. Cut the tomatoes into wedges and use to garnish the dish.

Potato, celery and cheese salad   *Serves 4–6*

The celery adds crunch to this salad and the Edam cheese makes it more nourishing.

450g (1 lb) boiled potatoes
6 tbsp French dressing
1 small head celery, chopped
1 large dessert apple, quartered, cored and diced
150ml (5 fl. oz) home-made mayonnaise
salt and pepper
175g (6 oz) Edam cheese, cut in slim wedges
1 tbsp chopped chives

Slice the potatoes into a bowl whilst still hot and then blend in the French dressing and leave on one side until quite cold. Then add the celery and apple with the mayonnaise and seasoning to taste. Leave in a cool place until required and then spoon onto a flat dish and arrange the Edam cheese around the edge of the dish and sprinkle the salad with chives.

Dutch salad   *Serves 4*

The cheese is best added just before tossing the salad. This salad may be served on individual dishes or in one large bowl.

1 cos lettuce cut in 5cm (2 in.) lengths
1 clove garlic, crushed
8 tbsp French dressing
3 tomatoes, skinned, quartered and pipped
½ cucumber, peeled and diced
225g (8 oz) French beans, cooked and cut in 3.5cm (1½ in.) lengths
1 small green pepper, quartered, pipped and thinly sliced
1 small onion, finely chopped
1 can anchovy fillets
2 hard-boiled eggs
75g (3 oz) Gouda cheese, diced

Arrange the lettuce leaves in the bottom of a salad bowl or serving dishes. Add the garlic to the French dressing, and the tomatoes, cucumber, beans, pepper and onion to the dressing with the anchovy fillets, toss lightly and then place on top of the lettuce. Cut the eggs in quarters lengthwise and arrange over the salad with the cheese and stir very lightly to mix so that the egg does not break up.

Keep fit salad   *Serves 2*

A low-calorie salad which can be followed with a crisp apple or large orange.

225g (8 oz) cottage cheese
4 spring onions, chopped
¼ level tsp dried dill
¼ level tsp freshly ground black pepper
100g (4 oz) shelled prawns
1 small green pepper, seeded and sliced
1 lemon cut in 8 wedges
2 heads chicory

Blend together the cottage cheese, spring onions, dill and pepper. Coarsely chop most of the prawns and add to the cheese mixture. Arrange the green pepper rings, lemon wedges and chicory leaves on two individual plates and then pile the cheese mixture on top and garnish with the remaining whole prawns.

Spicy cheese and carrots   *Serves 4*

225g (8 oz) cottage cheese
225g (8 oz) young new carrots
1 rounded tbsp chopped spring onions or chives
2 tsp Worcestershire sauce
salt
freshly ground black pepper

Put the cheese in a bowl. Wash the carrots and then top and tail and coarsely grate into a bowl, add the spring onions, Worcestershire sauce, salt and plenty of black pepper and stir well. Cover and leave in the refrigerator for at least an hour for the flavours to blend. Serve on a bed of lettuce and watercress.

Pineapple and cheese salad   *Serves 4*

225g (8 oz) cottage cheese
225g (8 oz) can pineapple titbits
a good pinch cayenne pepper
salt

Place the cottage cheese in a bowl. Thoroughly drain the pineapple and stir into the cheese with the cayenne and salt. Cover and leave in the refrigerator for at least an hour for the flavours to blend. Serve on a bed of lettuce and chicory.

Cottage cheese and fruit salad   *Serves 4*

2 oranges, peeled and sliced
4 rings pineapple
220g (8 oz) can or fresh peach halves, drained
450g (16 oz) cottage cheese
lettuce, watercress and chicory

Place the fruit together in a bowl and mix lightly. Season the cottage cheese lightly.
    Arrange the lettuce, watercress and chicory on a flat serving dish and pile the cheese down the centre, spoon the fruit around the edge. Serve with French bread or crusty rolls.

French dressing *Makes about 300ml (10 fl. oz)*

½ clove garlic, crushed
½–1 level tsp salt
plenty of freshly ground black pepper
1 level tsp very finely chopped onion
3 level tsp caster sugar
150ml (5 fl. oz) olive, vegetable or corn oil
4–6 tbsp cider or white wine vinegar
1 level tsp dry mustard

Place all the dry ingredients together in a small bowl and with a whisk or wooden spoon beat in the oil and vinegar until well blended and smooth. Taste and check seasoning and use as required.

Mayonnaise *Makes about 300ml (10 fl. oz)*

2 egg yolks
1 level tsp made mustard
1 level tsp salt
pepper
1 level tsp caster sugar
1 tbsp white wine or cider vinegar
300ml (10 fl. oz) corn or vegetable oil
1 tbsp lemon juice

Stand a bowl on a damp cloth to prevent it slipping on the table. Put the yolks, mustard, salt, pepper and sugar into a bowl with the vinegar and mix well. Add the oil drop by drop, beating well with a whisk the entire time until the mixture is smooth and thick. In order that the oil may be added a drop at a time, put into the bottle neck a cork from which a small wedge has been cut. Beat in the lemon juice.

Cheesecakes

and desserts

Cheesecake has a long pedigree. Roman emperors feasted on it; it was a feature of medieval banquets (King Richard II in fifteenth century England enjoyed a version flavoured with elderflowers). Today it is an honoured part of Central Euopean cookery – many English recipes are of German origin – and it is beloved in America where spice and often dried fruit are added; there are as many versions as there are flavours.

The favourite base today is made of crushed biscuit, whilst the filling is of eggs, cream, fruit, spice and above all the cheese that gives it its characteristic creamy consistency. It can be cream cheese, curd cheese, cottage cheese, or a mixture of all three. Fruit of all kinds may be used, either fresh or canned. Sometimes yogurt is added to the mixture.

Cheesecakes can be served cold or hot, they may be sweet or savoury, large or small. What they have in common is the crisp base and the contrasting rich, creamy filling. Some are baked and served hot, others are baked and served cold. Others are not cooked at all but chilled in the 'fridge. Variations use a pastry base to make a delicious form of tart. Or you can use the creamy filling mixture on its own, set in a mould and very well chilled.

Try some of these recipes for an impressive dinner party dessert, or for a family treat.

Pineapple cheesecake tarts *Makes 12*

Best served warm straight from the oven.

Pastry
100g (4 oz) plain flour
50g (2 oz) butter
2 tsp cold water
1 egg yolk
12½g (½ oz) caster sugar

Filling
1 egg
50g (2 oz) caster sugar
2 level tsp plain flour
100g (4 oz) cream cheese
225g (8 oz) crushed pineapple, thoroughly drained

Heat the oven to 190°C (375°F), gas mark 5.

Put the flour in a bowl, cut the butter in small pieces and rub in with the fingertips until it resembles fine breadcrumbs. Blend the water with the egg yolk. Stir the sugar into the flour and then add the water and egg mixture and bind together. Turn out onto a lightly floured table and knead lightly and then roll out and use to line 12 individual tart tins and prick the base thoroughly with a fork.

To make the fillings, blend the egg, sugar and flour together and then beat in the cream cheese and pineapple. Divide the mixture between the tarts and bake for 20 to 25 minutes or until the pastry is a pale golden brown and the filling set.

Raspberry and redcurrant cheesecake *Serves 6–8*

This recipe makes redcurrants and raspberries go a long way and is utterly delicious.

Flan case
100g (4 oz) digestive biscuits, crushed
25g (1 oz) caster sugar
50g (2 oz) butter, melted

Filling
450g (1 lb) cream cheese
100g (4 oz) caster sugar
2 eggs
grated rind and juice of 1 lemon

Topping
225g (8 oz) redcurrants
225g (8 oz) raspberries
75g (3 oz) caster sugar
4 tbsp water
1 rounded tsp arrowroot

Heat the oven to 180°C (350°F), gas mark 4 and butter a 20cm (8 in.) loose-bottomed cake tin or a spring-form tin.

First prepare the base. Blend the biscuits, sugar and melted butter together for the flan case and spread over the base of the tin.

To make the filling, mash the cheese until soft and then beat in the sugar, eggs and lemon rind and juice. Turn into the tin and bake for 1 to 1¼ hours or until the cheeesecake is set. Turn off the heat and leave to cool in the oven until quite cold.

For the topping, put the fruit in a pan with the sugar and water and bring slowly to the boil and simmer for 2 minutes. Drain the fruit thoroughly and spoon onto the cheesecake. Measure 150ml (5 fl. oz) of the fruit syrup and blend with the arrowroot, return to the pan and bring to the boil, stirring until thickened, then spoon over the fruit. Leave to set in the tin until required, then remove and place on a serving dish. Serve with single cream.

Swiss pineapple cheesecake   *Serves 8–10*

Serve very cold, decorated with pieces of pineapple and small sprigs of lemon balm.

Base
40g (1½ oz) margarine
100g (4 oz) digestive biscuits
40g (1½ oz) caster sugar

Filling
440g (15½ oz) can pineapple rings
225g (8 oz) rich cream cheese
50g (2 oz) caster sugar
2 eggs, separated
25g (1 oz) flour

Topping
150ml (5 fl. oz) soured cream
50g (2 oz) caster sugar
lemon balm to decorate

Heat the oven to 180°C (350°F), gas mark 4 and grease a 20–22.5cm (8–9 in.) cake tin with a loose base.

First prepare the base. Melt the margarine in a saucepan, crush the biscuits and add with the sugar and press onto the base of the tin.

To make the filling, drain the pineapple rings, reserving some pineapple for decoration, chop the remainder. Beat the cream cheese with one tablespoon pineapple juice until soft and gradually add the caster sugar and egg yolks, beating well. Fold in the chopped pineapple with the flour. Whisk the egg whites until stiff and fold into the mixture. Turn into the tin and bake in the oven for 1 hour or until set. For the toppings, mix together the soured cream and caster sugar, remove the cheesecake from the oven and spread over the topping. Return to the oven and reduce the heat to 150°C (300°F), gas mark 2 and cook for a further 15 minutes. Remove from the oven and leave to cool in the tin. When quite cold remove from the tin and place on a serving dish and decorate with the remaining pineapple and small pieces of lemon balm.

Blackberry cheesecake *Serves 8–10*

Blackberries make a delicious cheesecake with a good flavour. This cheesecake is made with the crust on top to start with. It is then turned out of the cake tin so that the crust base comes underneath, a good tip when you haven't a spring-form tin.

Filling
450g (1 lb) blackberries
175g (6 oz) caster sugar
3 tbsp cold water
12½g (½ oz) gelatine
350g (12 oz) cream cheese
2 eggs, separated
150ml (5 fl. oz) double cream

Base
100g (4 oz) digestive biscuits, crushed
25g (1 oz) demerara sugar
50g (2 oz) butter, melted

Pick over the blackberries and place in a saucepan with 100g (4 oz) caster sugar over a low heat to draw the juices out and dissolve the sugar, then simmer gently for about 5 minutes or until the fruit is tender.

Meanwhile place the cold water in a basin, sprinkle on the gelatine and leave to stand for 3 minutes, then draw the pan of fruit from the heat and stir in the gelatine until dissolved. Sieve the fruit into a bowl to make a purée and leave to cool until it starts to set. Cream the cheese with the egg yolks and remaining sugar and stir into the setting purée. Whisk the cream until thick. Whisk the egg whites with an electric or rotary hand whisk until stiff and then fold the cream and lastly the egg whites into the blackberry mixture. Turn into a 20cm (8 in.) cake tin with the base lightly oiled and lined with greaseproof paper and chill in the refrigerator for an hour.

Mix together the crushed biscuits, demerara sugar and melted butter and spread over the cheesecake. Leave to chill for a further 2 hours, preferably longer, before turning out. Dip the tin in very hot water for a moment to loosen the set and then turn out onto a serving dish.

Yorkshire cheesecake   *Serves 8*

A cooked cheesecake with a delicious lemon flavour.

Pastry

100g (4 oz) plain flour   juice of 1½ lemons
50g (2 oz) butter   cold water

Filling

225g (8 oz) curd or cream cheese   2 level tsp cornflour
50g (2 oz) caster sugar   2 tbsp double cream
2 eggs   1 tbsp melted butter
grated rind of 1 lemon   25g (1 oz) raisins

Heat the oven to 220°C (425°F), gas mark 7 and place a baking sheet in it.

To make the pastry place the flour in a bowl with the butter cut in small pieces and rub in with the fingertips until the mixture resembles fine breadcrumbs, then add the juice of half a lemon and just sufficient cold water to bind. Turn onto a lightly floured table, knead lightly and then roll out thinly and use to line a 22.5cm (9 in.) flan dish. Line the flan with a piece of greaseproof paper, weigh down with baking beans and bake blind for 10 minutes.

Meanwhile beat the cheese in a bowl with the sugar, eggs, grated lemon rind and remaining lemon juice until smooth, then blend the cornflour with the cream and stir into the mixture with the melted butter.

Remove the paper and beans from the flan and pour in the filling, sprinkle over the raisins and return to the oven, reduce the temperature to 180°C (350°F), gas mark 4 and bake for a further 30 minutes or until the cheesecake is set and pale golden brown.

Orange cheesecake   *Serves 6–8*

This can be made in a 20cm (8 in.) cake tin without a loose bottom. Then put the biscuit crust on top of the made cheesecake mixture so that as you turn it out of the cake tin the crust is underneath; this means that the crust is always crisp too.

Filling

12½g (½ oz) gelatine
150ml (5 fl. oz) cold water
175g (6 oz) can concentrated
  frozen orange juice, thawed
350g (12 oz) rich cream cheese
100g (4 oz) caster sugar
150ml (5 fl. oz) double cream, whipped

Biscuit base
50g (2 oz) ginger biscuits, crushed
50g (2 oz) digestive biscuits, crushed
25g (1 oz) demerara sugar
50g (2 oz) butter, melted
fresh orange segments
    to decorate

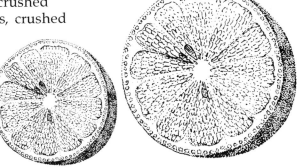

Soak the gelatine in the cold water for about 5 mintues, then stand in a
bowl in a pan of simmering water and leave until the gelatine has
dissolved and become quite clear. Remove from the heat, add the orange
juice and leave to become cold and nearly set.

Mix the cream cheese with the sugar and a little of the thick but not set
orange juice. Beat well and add the rest of the orange juice, mixing well.
Lastly fold in the whipped cream. Turn into a 20cm (8 in.) cake tin with
the base lightly greased, then lined with a circle of greaseproof paper. Chill
in the refrigerator until set.

To prepare the base, mix together the crushed biscuits, demerara sugar
and butter and spread over the cheesecake and chill for a further hour. Dip
the tin in very hot water for a moment to loosen the set cheesecake and
then turn out and decorate with fresh orange segments.

Cream cheese hearts   *Serves 4–8*

This is best served well chilled with extra cream. Both fresh strawberries
and raspberries are delicious with it. It is the dish that the French call
Coeurs à la crème.

450g (1 lb) cottage cheese
150ml (5 fl. oz) soured cream
2 tbsp icing sugar, sieved
¼ tsp salt

Sieve the cottage cheese, or purée in the blender. Beat the soured cream,
sugar and salt together and stir in the cheese. Turn the mixture into four
175g (6 oz) heart-shaped moulds lined with a double thickness of damp
muslin. Pack the mixture in tightly, and squeeze the liquid out through the
muslin and pour off the surplus liquid. Squeeze frequently and chill
overnight in the refrigerator.

Unmould onto a serving plate, remove the muslin and serve with fresh
strawberries, sugar and thick cream.

Strawberry cream cheese tartlets *Makes 12–15*

This is a good way to make a few strawberries go a long way – ideal for a coffee morning.

Pastry
100g (4 oz) plain flour
50g (2 oz) butter
25g (1 oz) caster sugar
1 egg yolk
2 tsp approx. cold water to mix

Filling
100g (4 oz) cream cheese
12½g (½ oz) butter
1 level tbsp caster sugar
a few drops of vanilla essence
225g (8 oz) small strawberries
2 rounded tbsp redcurrant jelly

To make the pastry place the flour in a bowl and add the butter cut in small pieces and rub in with the fingertips until it resembles fine breadcrumbs, then stir in the sugar. Blend the egg yolk with the water and stir into the flour and mix together with a knife until blended. Turn onto a floured table and knead lightly until smooth and then roll out thinly and use to line 12 to 15 tartlet tins. Prick each base well and then chill for 15 minutes. Heat the oven to 200°C (400°F), gas mark 6 and then bake the tarts in the centre for about 10 minutes or until the pastry is a pale golden brown around the edge. Lift out and leave to cool on a wire rack.

Meanwhile prepare the filling. Place the cream cheese, butter and sugar in a bowl and beat well until smooth and creamy then add vanilla essence taste. Place a spoonful in the base of each tart.

Hull the strawberries and arrange about three on the top of each tart, if they are large cut in half. Place the jam in a small saucepan and heat gently until melted then carefully brush over the strawberries to glaze. Leave in a cool place until required.

Cheesebread and scones

What is rich, golden, and smells delicious? The answer is, cheesebread hot from the oven. If the smell is not enough to tempt the appetite, the taste most certainly will. Bread and cheese go together like ham and eggs. What could be more natural than to bake them together?

Use grated Parmesan, Cheddar or odds and ends of any hard cheese you have in the larder. Add it to the basic bread or scone mixture and discover a whole new dimension in your baking. Serve cheesebread with a bowl of good vegetable soup and you have a meal, or with salad to make a light summer lunch. Make tiny rolls for coffee mornings food-with-a-difference. Add it to scones and baps. Use it grated into pastry mixture for cheese straws or biscuits to serve with drinks.

It makes a good loaf for cutting sandwiches to take on picnics – with egg and tomato filling, for instance, or perhaps with fruit like dates or bananas. Full of nourishing goodness, it is an ideal snack for ever-hungry children – and they love it.

And it goes beautifully with a glass of wine.

Cheese and herb scones   *Makes 10–12*

Serve these delicious scones for a coffee morning or with a cheese bread BOARD instead of biscuits or French bread.

225g (8 oz) self-raising flour
1 level tsp baking powder
pinch salt
50g (2 oz) butter, softened
75g (3 oz) full-flavoured Cheddar cheese, GRATED.
1 level tsp dry mustard
1 level tbsp chopped fresh herbs
1 egg
milk

Heat the oven to 220°C (425°F), gas mark 7 and lightly grease a baking sheet.

Sift the flour, baking powder and salt into a bowl and add the butter and rub in with the fingertips until the mixture resembles fine breadcrumbs. Stir in the cheese, mustard and herbs.

Crack the egg into a measuring jug and lightly beat and make up to 150ml (5 fl. oz) with milk, stir into the flour and mix to a soft dough. Turn onto a lightly floured table, knead gently and roll out to 1.25cm (½ in.) thickness and cut into rounds with a 5cm (2 in.) plain cutter to make 10 to 12 scones. Place on the baking sheet so that the scones just touch, brush with a little milk and bake for 10 minutes or until a pale golden brown. Remove from the baking sheet and leave to cool on a wire rack.

Cheese loaf

This bread keeps well and is especially good toasted or used as a base for snacks and sandwiches.

just under 300ml (10 fl. oz)
  hand-hot water
1 tsp sugar
2 level tsp dried yeast
450g (1 lb) strong white flour

2 level tsp salt
1 level tsp dry mustard
100–175g (4–6 oz) full-flavoured
  Cheddar cheese, grated

Dissolve the sugar in the water, sprinkle on the yeast and leave for 10 to 15 minutes until frothy.

Put the flour in a large bowl and add the salt, mustard and most of the cheese, keep a little on one side for sprinkling on the loaf before baking. Pour the yeast liquid into the bowl and mix well until the dough leaves the sides of the bowl clean. Turn onto a floured table and knead until smooth and no longer sticky; this will take about 10 minutes and is done by folding the dough towards you, then pushing down with the palm of the hand. Give the dough a quarter turn, repeat kneading, using a rocking rhythm, and continue until the dough feels firm and elastic. Shape into a large ball, place in a greased polythene bag and leave in a warm place to rise until doubled in bulk. This will take about 2 hours at room temperature or 1 hour in a warm place. Alternatively it may be left overnight in the refrigerator, in which case the dough must be allowed to return to room temperature before shaping.

Turn the dough onto a lightly floured table and flatten with the knuckles to knock out all the air and roll up like a Swiss roll and place in a greased loaf tin 19.5 × 10 × 6cm approx. (7¾ × 4 × 2½ in.). Put inside an oiled polythene bag and leave at room temperature until the dough rises to the top of the tin. Sprinkle with the remaining cheese and bake in the oven at 190°C (375°F), gas mark 5 for 45 minutes. When the loaf is done it will have shrunk from the sides of the tin and will be a deep golden brown. To test tap bread on the base: if ready it will sound hollow.

Cheese bread rolls   *Makes 8*

Easy to make, these are ideal to serve with a hot soup or to take on a picnic filled with egg and tomato.

283g (10 oz) packet white bread mix
175g (6 oz) full-flavoured Cheddar cheese, grated
225ml (7 fl. oz) hand-hot water

Put the bread mix in a bowl with 150g (5 oz) of the cheese, stir in the water and mix together to form a dough. Turn onto a lightly floured table and knead lightly for 5 minutes or until smooth and elastic. Divide into eight equal pieces and then shape into rolls, place on a greased baking sheet and put inside a large polythene bag and leave in a warm place for about 35 to 45 minutes or until doubled in bulk. Whilst the bread is rising heat the oven to 230°C (450°F), gas mark 8.
   Sprinkle the remaining cheese over the rolls and bake in the oven for 10 to 15 minutes or until well risen and golden brown.

Cheese and tomato whirls   *Makes 16*

Best served warm straight from the oven.

225g (8 oz) self-raising flour
50g (2oz) butter
½ level tsp dry mustard powder
100g (4 oz) full-flavoured Cheddar
   cheese, grated
salt and pepper
4 tbsp milk
1 egg, beaten
4 rashers streaky bacon
2–3 tbsp tomato purée

Heat the oven to 220°C (425°F), gas mark 7. Well butter a large baking tray.
   Put the flour in a bowl and rub in the butter until the mixture resembles breadcrumbs. Add the mustard, half of the cheese and seasoning and mix well. Blend the milk with the egg, stir into the mixture and use to bind to a soft dough.
   Remove the rind and bone from the bacon and cut into thin strips. Fry gently for 3 to 4 minutes to allow the fat to run out and drain well.
   Roll out the dough on a lightly floured table to an oblong about 35 × 17.5cm approx. (14 × 7 in.). Spread with the tomato purée and then sprinkle on the remaining cheese and bacon pieces. Roll up the dough Swiss roll fashion starting from the longest side. Moisten the edge with a

little milk and seal. Cut into 16 slices and place on the baking tray, cut-side down. Bake for about 15 minutes or until golden brown.

Cheese drop scones *Makes 16–18*

Adding Parmesan cheese to the basic drop scone mixture, makes a change and gives a delicious flavour. Serve warm with butter.

100g (4 oz) self-raising flour
¼ level tsp salt
20g (¾ oz) Parmesan cheese, grated
½ level tsp dry mustard
1 egg
150ml (5 fl. oz) milk

Place the flour in a bowl with the salt, cheese and mustard powder, stir lightly to mix then make a well in the centre of the flour and crack in the egg. Using a wooden spoon, gradually mix in the milk. Stir thoroughly from the centre, drawing in the flour from the outer edges; this will form a fairly thick batter.

Place a large, heavy flat-based frying pan over a moderate heat. Rub over the surface with a piece of kitchen paper dipped in a little oil. Place the mixture in tablespoonfuls onto the hot surface, only about four at a time and well spaced apart. When the bubbles have risen to the surface and the underside is brown, loosen and turn over. Cook for a minute or so on the second side, then lift from the pan and cool in a folded tea towel.

Rub over the surface again and continue to make the scones until all the batter is used up. Serve with plenty of butter whilst still warm.

Party fare and savouries

Cheese in party mood is the hostess's best friend. Cheese goes naturally with wine to make entertaining easy, relaxed and informal. All the preparations, including any cooking required, are done beforehand and you are free to look after your guests without wondering with half your mind just what is going on in the kitchen.

For a simple wine and cheese party, stick to one brand of red and one of white wine, allowing about half or three quarters of a bottle to each guest. Provide a limited number of cheeses that can be cut into, rather than a lot of little pieces. You will need an interesting variety of bread, rolls, crispbreads and biscuits. Have plenty of garnishes – watercress, radishes, cocktail onions, gherkins, pickles. Fruit too – apples, pears and grapes are particularly happy with cheese. And *do* have some prepared dishes and savouries, which do so much for the festive spirit.

Make a bowl or two of cheese dip and serve it with savoury biscuits, celerly, cauliflower sprigs, potato crisps. This, with a selection of savouries, some hot if posible, can be the centrepiece of the party.

For a special occasion try a cheese fondue. In Switzerland where it was invented this is *the* party dish. The hostess prepares it at table and the guests gather round to dip pieces of bread into it. For this a supply of long fondue forks is advisable, and French bread.

Presentation of party food is half the battle. Savouries, which can also be served as appetisers with drinks before dinner, are full of decorative possibilities. Remember they should be small, plentiful, and as attractive as you can make them.

Mild curry and mustard dip

A very delicious dip, the remains of which can be used as a sandwich filling with a little watercress.

225g (8 oz) rich cream cheese
4 level tbsp mango chutney sauce
½ level tsp dry mustard
1 level tsp curry powder

Mix all the ingredients together until thoroughly blended and then turn into a serving dish and leave to stand in a cool place for an hour or two to allow the flavours to blend. Serve with crisps or small sticks of celery.

Crab dip

A lovely creamy dip, to be served with savoury biscuits and crisps or thin fingers of celery and carrot with small sprigs of raw cauliflower.

3 tbsp yogurt
1 level tbsp tomato ketchup
1 tbsp lemon juice
a good pinch cayenne pepper
salt
175g (6 oz) rich cream cheese
198g (7 oz) can crab meat

Put the yogurt, ketchup, lemon juice, cayenne and salt with the cream cheese in a blender and purée until smooth.

Drain the crab meat, remove any bones and add to the blender and purée for just a very short while to blend with the cheese so that the crab meat is just chopped. Turn into a small dish, cover with foil and chill thoroughly for at least 2 to 3 hours to allow the flavours to blend.

Horseradish and cheese dip

Serve with potato crisps or thin fingers of celery.

175g (6 oz) cream cheese
1 level tbsp chopped chives
2 level tbsp creamed horseradish
3–4 level tbsp mayonnaise, home-made
  (see page 92) or a good bought variety
freshly ground black pepper

Cream the cheese until soft and then beat in the remaining ingredients. Turn into a small bowl, cover with foil and chill for at least an hour before serving.

Garlic cheese

Serve this as a spread on canapés or include it on a cheese board with a selection of other cheese.

225g (8 oz) cream cheese
1 clove garlic
salt
1 tbsp finely chopped chives
1 level tbsp finely chopped parsley

Cream the cheese in a bowl until soft. Crush the garlic with a little salt using the blade of a knife until a smooth paste, then add to the bowl with no extra salt. If you have a garlic press, squeeze the juice straight into the bowl of cheese and add a little salt. Add the chives and parsley and mix thoroughly. Spoon the mixture into a dish and then cover with foil or cling film and chill for several hours to allow the flavours to develop.

Potted Stilton

Provided that fresh Stilton is used this will keep in the refrigerator for a month. Otherwise, a very good way of using up the last crumbly pieces of a Stilton. Use as a spread or serve in a small pot on the cheeseboard.

450g (1 lb) Stilton cheese
100g (4 oz) butter, softened
salt
port or Madeira

Place the Stilton in a bowl and mash thoroughly, then add the softened butter with the salt and beat thoroughly and moisten with a little port or Madeira. Press down well into one or two pots.

If using on a cheeseboard it is a good idea to melt a little extra butter and pour over the cheese to cover and seal. Chill well before serving.

Fresh herb cheese

This is something I very frequently do in the summer when my herbs are at their best. It must be made the day before so that the flavours have time to blend. The best herbs to use are fresh parsley, chives and a little marjoram and lemon thyme if available. Add garlic to suit your taste.

225g (8 oz) rich cream cheese
2 rounded tbsp chopped mixed
  fresh herbs
1 large clove garlic, crushed
single cream or top milk
freshly ground black pepper
salt

Place the cheese in a bowl with the herbs and garlic and beat well and then add sufficient cream or top milk to mix to a light cream. Add plenty of black pepper and salt to taste. Serve in a dish or piled straight onto the cheeseboard and sprinkled with a little extra chopped chives. This will keep for about 10 days in the refrigerator.

Camembert savoury

A different, almost home-made cheese.

75g (3 oz) Camembert or 3
  individual cheese portions
150g (5 oz) curd cheese
3 tbsp chopped parsley

Peel any hard skin off the Camembert and then mash with a fork in a bowl until smooth and then beat in the curd cheese. Cover the bowl and chill for an hour. Divide the mixture into six equal portions and shape each into a triangle. Coat with the chopped parsley, place on a serving dish and keep in a cool place until required. Serve with biscuits and butter or French bread.

Piped cheese savouries

These are so easy to prepare and are excellent served as appetisers before a meal or as a savoury at a party.

celery sticks
small rounds of fried bread
rich cream cheese
milk
salt
paprika
halved green grapes

Wash the celery and cut into neat lengths about 5cm (2 in.) long and lay with the fried bread on a flat dish.

Cream the cheese with a little milk until soft and a piping consistency, then add seasoning to taste. Place in a piping bag fitted with a large rose pipe and pipe into the celery sticks and in swirls on the bread. Sprinkle the celery with a little paprika and place a halved green grape on the small fried bread rounds.

Variations

The cream cheese may be prepared as above and used to pipe into halved tomatoes with the seeds scooped out and may be decorated with a few finely chopped chives.

Alternately cut a cucumber into 2.5cm (1 in.) lengths and scoop out some of the seeds in the centre and then pipe the cream cheese into the centre and garnish with a prawn or shrimp.

Avocado dip

This is very good and is best made on the day that it is needed as it discolours if kept too long.

4 ripe avocado pears
150ml (5 fl. oz) double cream
75g (3 oz) rich cream cheese
½ level tsp English made mustard
4 level tsp caster sugar
2 tbsp lemon juice
1 tsp cider vinegar
salt and black ground pepper
a little green colouring
small sprig watercress to garnish

Cut the avocadoes in half, remove the stones and scoop out the flesh, put in a bowl and mash with a fork until smooth. Blend together the cream and cheese and then stir into the avocado mixture. Season with the mustard, sugar, lemon juice, vinegar and plenty of salt and pepper. Add a few drops of green colouring if liked.

Pile into a dish and serve with crisps, cauliflower florets, carrot sticks and small sticks of celery and garnish the dish with a small sprig of watercress.

Cheese straws

Prepare these in advance and keep stored in an air-tight tin.

225g (8 oz) plain flour
salt and pepper
100g (4 oz) butter
100g (4 oz) full-flavoured Cheddar
  or Parmesan cheese, grated
a little beaten egg

Heat the oven to 200°C (400°F), gas mark 6. Lightly grease some baking sheets.

Put the flour in a bowl with the salt and pepper and add the butter cut in small pieces, rub in with the fingertips until the mixture resembles fine breadcrumbs, then stir in the cheese. Add sufficient beaten egg to make a firm dough, turn out onto a floured table and knead lightly until smooth. Roll out to approximately 0.6cm (¼ in.) thickness and cut the dough into narrow strips, rings, circles or any fancy shape required. Place on the baking sheets and bake for about 8 to 10 minutes or until a pale golden brown. Leave to cool on the baking sheets for a minute or two and then lift onto a wire rack to finish cooling.

Cheese aigrettes *Makes 16*

These are delicious served with drinks or they may be served as a savoury course.

25g (1 oz) butter
150ml (5 fl. oz) water
50g (2 oz) self-raising flour
1 egg + 1 egg yolk
50g (2 oz) full-flavoured Cheddar cheese, grated
salt
cayenne pepper

Put the butter and water in a small saucepan and bring to the boil. Remove from the heat and add the flour, beat well until the mixture is glossy and leaves the sides of the pan clean, then cool slightly.

Lightly mix the yolk and the egg together and beat into the mixture a little at a time. Stir in the cheese, salt and a pinch of cayenne pepper, and check seasoning. When required, drop the mixture in heaped teaspoonfuls into hot deep fat and fry gently until golden brown, turning once. Lift out with a slotted spoon and drain on kitchen paper and then serve at once.

Variation

If liked add 25g (1 oz) finely chopped Camembert cheese instead of 25g (1 oz) of Cheddar. This is a good way of using up the ends of a piece of Camembert that has gone hard.

Savoury cheese balls

Serve these as a snack with drinks or use them to serve on the top of casseroles or savoury dishes. Children love them served with baked beans.

100g (4 oz) white breadcrumbs
100g (4 oz) full-flavoured Cheddar cheese, grated
1 level tbsp chopped parsley
1 small onion, finely grated
¼ level tsp mixed dried herbs
salt and pepper
1 egg, beaten

Put all the ingredients together in a bowl and mix thoroughly and shape the mixture into balls. Make small balls if using to serve with drinks or slightly larger if serving with a casserole or a savoury dish.

Put on a baking tray and bake in a moderate oven 190°C (375°F), gas mark 5 for about 35 to 40 minutes or until crisp and golden brown.

Mushroom appetizers *Makes 40–48*

Adding cream cheese to a pastry mix gives it a lovely flavour and texture.

Filling
50g (2 oz) butter
1 medium onion, very finely chopped
225g (8 oz) mushrooms, very finely chopped
salt and pepper
1 tbsp flour

Pastry
100g (4 oz) rich cream cheese
100g (4 oz) butter
350g (12 oz) self-raising flour
½ level tsp salt
beaten egg

Melt the butter in a saucepan, add the onion and cook gently for 5 minutes, then add the mushrooms and continue cooking for a further 5 minutes, then season well. Stir in the flour to thicken and cook for a minute, then remove from the heat and leave to cool.

Heat the oven to 180°C (350°F), gas mark 4.

Now prepare the pastry. Cream the cheese and butter together until soft and then work in the flour and salt to make a dough. Turn out onto a lightly floured table and knead lightly until smooth. Roll out thinly and cut into circles with a 7.5cm (3 in.) cutter. Damp the edges with a little beaten egg. Place a little filling on one half of each circle, then fold over the pastry and press the edges firmly together with a fork, place on a baking sheet and brush lightly with a little more beaten egg. Bake in the oven for 15 minutes or until golden brown. Serve warm.

Swiss cheese fondue *Serves 4*

The classic fondue is made from half Emmenthal and half Gruyère, but you can use the less expensive Jarlsburg cheese which has similar characteristics but is not quite so good. When stirring the fondue stir with a wooden spatula to prevent the fondue sticking to the base of the pan. In Switzerland they usually let the last amount of the fondue just catch on the botton until it is a pale brown crust, and this is then just eased off and tastes scrumptious.

To eat the fondue dip cubes of French bread on the end of the fork into it, twirl it around then enjoy yourself.

1 clove garlic, crushed
225g (8 oz) Emmenthal cheese, grated
225g (8 oz) Gruyère cheese, grated
4 glasses dry white wine
25g (1 oz) cornflour
salt
pepper
1 tbsp kirsch

Put the garlic, cheese and all but 3 tablespoons of the wine into a thick pan and heat the mixture very slowly until the cheese has dissolved. Do not let it boil.

Blend the cornflour with the remaining wine in a bowl until smooth, add a little of the hot cheese mixture to the cornflour and then stir it into the pan. Carefully bring the fondue to the boil, stirring all the time until the mixture has thickened. Add salt and pepper to taste, stir in the kirsch and serve at once.

Tapas are the eats that they serve in Spain with drinks, nicer than our usual canapés as they are not covered with aspic or served on soggy bread.

Olive nibblers   *Makes 12–16*

You may find that if the cheese is very moist there is no need to add milk. It is quite a sticky business rolling these balls but the result is well worth it.

100g (4 oz) cream cheese
1 tbsp milk
25g (1 oz) stuffed green olives, chopped
salt and pepper
50g (2 oz) mixed nuts, chopped very finely

Blend the cheese and milk, stir in the olives and add seasoning to taste. Form into small balls, roll in the chopped nuts and then chill in the refrigerator. Serve on cocktail sticks stuck into a tomato.

Cheese and olive puffs   *Makes 15*

These hot savouries are fiddly to make but a tasty mouthful. Best to bake and serve whilst still hot.

200g (7 oz) packet frozen puff pastry,
  just thawed or home-made (see next page)
1 egg, beaten
50g (2 oz) Gruyère cheese, thinly sliced
15 slices of stuffed green olives

Roll out the pastry to an oblong 37.5cm × 22.5cm approx. (15 × 9 in.) and cut it into squares, 7.5cm (3 in.) each side. Brush two edges of each square with beaten egg.
  Cut the cheese into 5cm (2 in.) squares, then in half to form triangles. Put one on each square of pastry and top with a slice of olive. Fold over the pastry and seal with a fork. Place on a baking sheet and brush with more egg and bake at 220°C (425°F), gas mark 7 for 10 to 15 minutes, until well risen and a pale golden brown.

Quick flaky or puff pastry

Equivalent to a small packet of bought puff pastry.

100g (4 oz) strong plain flour
½ tsp salt
75g (3 oz) hard margarine
about 4½ tbsp cold water

Sift the flour and salt into a mixing bowl. Coarsely grate the margarine in to the bowl. Stir in just sufficient water to make a firm dough and then roll out on a lightly floured surface to make a strip about 1.25cm (½ in.) thick and 15cm (6 in.) wide. Fold the pastry in three and give it a quarter turn to the left. Roll out again into a strip and fold in three.

   Wrap the pastry in foil and chill in the refrigerator for 30 minutes. Roll out the pastry on a floured table and use as required.

Spanish omelette slices

Cold Spanish omelette is moist and delicious. Use only firm tomatoes.

4 eggs
salt and pepper
1 tbsp olive oil
1 small onion, sliced
1 medium potato, peeled and diced
1 small green pepper, chopped
1 clove garlic, crushed
2 skinned tomatoes, quartered or
   cut in strips
1 thick slice ham, diced
25g (1 oz) Parmesan cheese

Lightly beat the eggs and add the salt and pepper. Heat the oil in an omelette pan. Add the onion and potato and fry lightly until softened but not browned, stir in the green pepper, garlic, tomatoes and ham and cook for a further 3 minutes. Pour in the egg mixture and cook quickly for 3 minutes until lightly browned on the under side. Sprinkle with the cheese and put under a hot grill to brown the top. Allow to cool slightly and then cut into small triangles.

Index